Denishawn:
the enduring influence

Denishawn:
the enduring influence

Jane Sherman

Twayne Publishers

Twayne's Dance Series

Don McDonagh, Editor

Choreographer and Composer:
Theatrical Dance and Music
in Western Culture by Baird Hastings

Denishawn: the enduring influence
by Jane Sherman

George Balanchine
by Don McDonagh

To
Miss Ruth and Papa
and
all their Denishawn Dancers,
past, present, and future

Denishawn:
the enduring influence

Jane Sherman

Copyright © 1983
by Jane Sherman
All Rights Reserved

Published in 1983
by Twayne Publishers
A Division of G. K. Hall & Company
70 Lincoln Street, Boston, Massachusetts 02111

Printed on permanent/durable
acid-free paper and bound in
the United States of America.

First Printing

44953

This book was designed by
Barbara Anderson and typeset
in Sabon by Compset, Inc.
with Snell roundhand display type supplied
by Typographic House.

Library of Congress Cataloging in Publication Data

Sherman, Jane, 1908–
Denishawn, the enduring influence.

(Twayne's dance series)
Bibliography p. 156
Includes index.
1. Denishawn School of Dance—History.
I. Title. II. Series
GV1786.D43S528   1983   793.3'2'0973   83-6099
ISBN 0-8057-9602-9

Contents

Editor's Foreword

DENISHAWN WAS QUITE SIMPLY the cradle of American modern dance if only because it provided the technical training and theatrical seasoning for Martha Graham, Doris Humphrey, and Charles Weidman. These three talented students, dancers, and choreographers became major figures who established modern dance as an artistic movement in the years between the two World Wars. By the 1940s and 1950s former members of their companies had separated to establish their own groups and create a geometric expansion in the number of modern dance troupes in this country. By the end of the decade of the 1950s, two dozen companies could trace their lineage to these so-called big three. It was a marked contrast to the early days of Denishawn between 1914 and 1930, when it alone was the company that presented serious concert dance, this at a time when the term "modern dance" had yet to be coined. Ironically, Denishawn's influence was almost totally ignored or lost sight of in the flowering process.

Denishawn itself had ceased as a performing entity in the beginning of 1932, although Ted Shawn and Ruth St. Denis each pursued independent careers that continued until their deaths in the late 1960s and early 1970s. It was only at the end of their long performing careers that their significance and that of Denishawn began once again to be recognized. This understanding and appreciation is a revisionary effort that is still in process.

For artistic reasons, which at the time may have seemed necessary and justified, Graham, Humphrey, and Weidman volubly rejected the sensibility of Denishawn when they embarked on their own creative journeys. Their work involved radical changes in the shapes of the dances they designed and resulted in a sharp turn to the academic community for supportive audiences, which sent down roots in university dance departments where modern dance developed into an accredited academic discipline.

By contrast, Denishawn had made its way in the rough and tumble of the commercial theater. It accepted all of the inevitable difficulties an artist encounters when trying to maintain the standards of art while at the same time appealing to a popular audience. The balance between the two was never entirely stable, as Denishawn veered between high seriousness and necessary froth in its programming. To their everlasting credit, Shawn and St. Denis never lost sight of their goal, which was to present intellectually stimulating fare in the language of dance. They considered it an honorable calling, even when their presentations were sandwiched between such vaudeville diversions as animal acts and comedy routines.

Principles of professionalism in terms of theatrical skills such as costuming, makeup, and lighting were always a hallmark of Denishawn, as was belief in the infinite expressive possibilities of the trained human body. The Denishawn Dancer was not an inspired amateur but a skilled performer whose regular attendance at dance class was a requisite for appearance on stage. Both Shawn and St. Denis were voracious readers with a special interest in religious and philosophical texts, and both were extremely receptive to the dance traditions and values of other cultures. The great Indian poet Rabindranath Tagore attributed the reawakened interest (by Indian intellectuals) in Indian dance to the influence of Denishawn. Shawn regularly read sections of philosophical or literary texts to the company as part of their cultural training. Significantly, Graham followed the same practice with her own company.

Graham, Humphrey, and Weidman all maintained strict professional standards in their own appearances and those of their companies', even as they were working through their own special artistic problems. The custom of making individual company members responsible for the care of their costumes was one they had experienced with Denishawn and one they continued when they declared their independence. In insisting on such practical details and in keeping the larger concept of dance as a serious artistic activity they drew on their Denishawn experience.

It would have been inconceivable that such dedicated individuals could have been attracted to Denishawn in the first place or have remained with Denishawn as long as they did (over ten years in Humphrey's case) if they had not sensed an essential integrity of purpose in its founders. The generations that followed these three inherited *their* integrity of purpose without ever quite understanding where its true origins lay.

At times, "popularity" was the only quality through which Denishawn could have survived as a dance force and it is on this aspect of Denishawn that most attention has been placed. However, it was never more than part of the story. The rounded picture presented by Jane Sherman in the following pages is a necessary corrective to persistent misconceptions about the role and importance of Denishawn as a cultural force in dance.

Her dedication and crusading zeal in writing, lecturing, and restaging Denishawn dances has in great measure brought about the current reevaluation of Denishawn's contribution. When seen, the dances can and do speak for their worth, but happily this crusader has also taken the time to assemble and write down essential historical information. It is derived primarily from her own first-hand experience as a student and dancer with Denishawn and secondarily from those surviving companions in that special community known as Denishawn Dancers.

Don McDonagh

Preface

IT IS NOT ALWAYS POSSIBLE to state a simple reason for writing a book, because the drive that impels one to the typewriter is often made up of conflicting aims. Yet I believe the title of this work expresses my purpose: I seek to explain how Denishawn became an enduring influence on American modern dance.

I do this primarily, although not exclusively, on the basis of my own experiences as a Denishawn student and company member for five years, using the insight gained thereby to clarify certain misconceptions that still persist about Denishawn and its leaders. These misconceptions are understandable, given the fact that following the personal and professional separation of Ruth St. Denis and Ted Shawn in 1931, the institution they had founded suffered an eclipse that lasted almost forty years.

Up to the mid-1970s, researchers and the general public could gain a glimpse of that institution only through the partial autobiographies of St. Denis (*An Unfinished Life*) and Shawn (*One Thousand and One Night Stands*), Walter Terry's biographies (*Miss Ruth,* and *Ted Shawn: Father of American Dance*), Dr. Christena L. Schlundt's *Chronology of the Professional Appearances and Dances of Ruth St. Denis and Ted Shawn,* and my own book (*Soaring: The Diary and Letters of a Denishawn Dancer in the Far East: 1925–1926*). Not until performers presented their reconstructions of a few long-neglected dances did a wider interest in Denishawn begin to revive, and present-day audiences saw for the first time examples of works that proved that institution's historical importance.

As a "survivor" I was stimulated by this unexpected renaissance. I wrote another book *(The Drama of Denishawn Dance)* and many articles on Denishawn. I started a steady correspondence with the handful of newly located fellow survivors. I plagued with lengthy letters those editors and authors who in my opinion were misinterpreting the methods of St. Denis and Shawn or underestimating the contribution that they and their Denishawn Dancers had made to dance. It is a contribution that continued through the great period of Denishawn (1922–1931), through Shawn's Men Dancers (1933–1940), and, more significantly, through the choreography and teachings of St. Denis's and Shawn's most famous pupils, Graham, Humphrey, and Weidman, even to their descendents right up to today. It is at last being granted the recognition it so justly merits.

In her doctoral dissertation, Betty Poindexter of Texas Women's University included a poignant quote from Ted Shawn:

Power with words ... things I have felt but could never express in words. Particularly the ephemeral quality of the dance has been a tragic ache in me always. It is a strange paradox that I who have a strong desire for what will endure, and will be permanent, should have chosen the art form which leaves nothing but memories, and these fade so swiftly, and with the death of the one who remembers, all is gone. And yet, I am satisfied this is my medium and my destiny.

It is my hope that with the "power of words" I can preserve in this volume aspects of Denishawn that might otherwise remain unexplored, so that "with the death of the one who remembers" all will not be completely "gone."

Jane Sherman

Acknowledgments

I AM ESPECIALLY GRATEFUL to my editor, Don McDonagh, for his patience and understanding; to Suzanne Shelton for her sharing of material; to Dr. Christena L. Schlundt for her thought-provoking correspondence; to my fellow Denishawn survivors Anne Douglas, Geordie Graham, and Gertrude Shurr for their loving support; to Barton Mumaw, my dear friend in writing and in the dance for his unfailing help; and, as always, to my husband, Ned Lehac, without whom—

Portions of some chapters of this book first appeared in an altered form in *Ballet Review, Dance Chronicle,* and *Dance Magazine,* and are used with the permission of editors Francis Mason, George Dorris, and Richard Philp, to whom the author expresses her thanks.

Chronology

1879   Ruth St. Denis born, January 20, in Eagleswood, New Jersey.

1891   Ted Shawn born, October 21, in Kansas City, Missouri.

1893   St. Denis makes her debut as a dancer at Somerset Hall, Somerville, New Jersey.

1906   St. Denis makes her New York City debut as a professional soloist at the New York Theatre, performing *Radha, Incense,* and *The Cobras,* January 28.

1906–1909   St. Denis performs her Oriental works in London, Paris, Berlin, Prague, Vienna, Dusseldorf, Hamburg, Brussels, Dresden, Budapest, Nuremburg, Graz, Monte Carlo, Munich, Breslau, Wiesbaden, Baden-Baden, Weimar, Cologne, Bonn, Edinburgh, and Glasgow.

1908–1909   Ted Shawn exercises to recover from paralysis of his legs, and begins to study dancing.

1909   St. Denis returns to the United States and, on the basis of her European success, is booked for a tour of the eastern states.

1910   St. Denis presents her first full-length dance drama *Egypta* at the New Amsterdam Theatre in New York City, December 12.

1911   St. Denis performs society and vaudeville dates. Shawn first sees her when she dances *Egypta* in Denver, Colorado.

1913   Shawn makes his debut as a dancer, performing ballroom dances on tours with his partner, Norma Gould.

1914   Shawn goes to New York, auditions for St. Denis, and is engaged as her partner.

Ruth St. Denis and Ted Shawn are married in New York City, August 13.

1914–1915   First United States tour of St. Denis and Shawn after their marriage, August 19 to February 21.

1915   Establishment in the summer of the first Denishawn school under the name of the Ruth St. Denis School of Dancing and Its Related Arts, Los Angeles.

1915–1916   Concert and vaudeville tour, October–May, of Ruth St. Denis, assisted by Ted Shawn and a company of eleven. Louis Horst becomes their first musical director.

1916   Name of school changed to Denishawn during the summer. Martha Graham enrolls as a pupil.
First appearance of dancers, July 29, in the Greek Theatre of the University of California in Berkeley, when St. Denis and Shawn and a large company present *A Dance Pageant of Egypt, Greece, and India.* Graham here makes her Denishawn debut as an ensemble dancer. Shawn choreographs his first all-male work, *The Pyrrhic Dance,* as part of the pageant.

1916–1917   Ruth St. Denis, Ted Shawn, and their Denishawn Dancers tour the Orpheum vaudeville circuit.

1917   Shawn enlists in United States Army Ambulance Corps. Doris Humphrey and Pauline Lawrence enter the Denishawn School.

1918   Ruth St. Denis tours, January–June, in vaudeville with Louis Horst as musical director.

1918–1919   St. Denis, assisted by Doris Humphrey and three other dancers, with Louis Horst, tours, November–September, Pantages vaudeville circuit from coast to coast and back.

1919   Shawn produces for vaudeville the three-act *Julnar of the Sea,* featuring Lillian Powell, with ten other dancers. Charles Weidman comes to the Denishawn School.

1919–1920   Tour of the Ruth St. Denis Concert Dancers, featuring Doris Humphrey, with Pauline Lawrence at the piano, and St. Denis and Shawn as guest stars.

1920   Shawn opens the Ted Shawn Studio in Los Angeles, April 6.

1921   Shawn produces for vaudeville the two-act *Xochitl,* featuring Martha Graham, with Charles Weidman. Pauline Lawrence at the piano. Martha's sister Georgia joins the Denishawn Dancers.

St. Denis and Shawn tour, January–May, in concert with actor Craig Ward and pianist Ann Thompson.

Shawn tours, September–December, cross-country with Martha Graham, Betty May, Dorothea Bowen, and Charles Weidman. Louis Horst at the piano.

1922   St. Denis and Shawn, with Martha Graham, Weidman, three other dancers, and Horst, make a brief United States concert tour, then appear in vaudeville in London, Manchester, and Bristol, England, for two months.

1922–1923   Impresario Daniel Mayer books the first of three United States concert tours for St. Denis, Shawn, and their Denishawn Dancers, including Martha Graham, Weidman, and Louise Brooks, with Horst as musical director.

1923–1924   Second Mayer tour for St. Denis, Shawn, and their Denishawn Dancers, including Doris Humphrey, Georgia (Geordie) Graham, Brooks, and Lawrence, with Horst as musical director.

1924–1925   Third Mayer tour for St. Denis, Shawn, and their Denishawn Dancers, with Humphrey, Weidman, Lawrence, G. Graham, Anne Douglas, and others. Horst as musical director.

1925   First concert appearances, July 14–15, at New York City's Lewisohn Stadium of St. Denis, Shawn, Humphrey, Weidman, Lawrence, and other Denishawn Dancers (including Jane Sherman). Horst leaves and Clifford Vaughan becomes musical director for Denishawn.

1925–1926   St. Denis, Shawn, and Denishawn Dancers Humphrey, Weidman, Lawrence, G. Graham, Jane Sherman, and others tour, August 1925–November 1926, Japan, China, Burma, India, [Pakistan], Ceylon, Malaya, Java, and the Philippines.

1926–1927   St. Denis, Shawn, and Denishawn Dancers Humphrey, Weidman, Lawrence, G. Graham, Sherman, and others tour the United States under the management of Arthur Judson. On evenings of April 4 and 5 and matinee and evening performances on April 6 they sell out Carnegie Hall for a record-breaking four successive concerts.

1927–1928   St. Denis, Shawn, G. Graham, Ernestine Day, Ronny Johansson, Sherman, and other Denishawn Dancers tour the United States for forty weeks as featured stars of the *Ziegfeld Follies*.

1928–1929   Second Lewisohn Stadium appearances for St. Denis, Shawn, and their Denishawn Dancers, August 20–22.

St. Denis, Shawn, and Denishawn Dancers tour the eastern states, October–March.

Shawn, with Denishawn Dancers, plays engagements in Atlantic City, New Jersey, and Jamaica and New Rochelle, New York, March–April.

St. Denis appears, April 7, with Ann Thompson McDowell, pianist, and the Mischa Gegna Concert Trio at the Los Angeles Figueroa Playhouse.

Shawn, assisted by the Khariton Duo and Simeon Spielmann, cellist, dances at Carnegie Hall, April 15.

Third Lewisohn Stadium concert, August 6–8, for St. Denis, Shawn, and their Denishawn Dancers. Hans Lange, conductor.

1929–1930   St. Denis and Shawn make a duet tour of the United States, assisted by a symphonic quartet.

Fourth Lewisohn Stadium concert, August 12–14, for St. Denis, Shawn, and the Denishawn Dancers.

1930–1932   Shawn and the Denishawn Dancers, including Jack Cole, make a United States tour, October 1930–February 1931.

Shawn appears in Berlin, Zurich, Berne, and Munich, March 1931–May 1931.

Fifth Lewisohn Stadium concert, August 24, 26, 28, 1931, for St. Denis, Shawn, and the Denishawn Dancers.

Ted Shawn and His Dancers, including Barton Mumaw, make a concert tour from New York City to Eustis, Florida, December 1931–March 1932.

This marks the end of the chronology for Denishawn, as Ruth St. Denis and Ted Shawn each went separate ways, each continuing active in the dance world to the end of their lives.

1968   Ruth St. Denis dies at age 89, July 21.

1972   Ted Shawn dies at age 80, January 9.

Chapter One
In The Beginning

THE "DENIS" WAS RUTH ST. DENIS, born Ruth Dennis on January 20, 1879, in Eagleswood, New Jersey. The "Shawn" was Ted Shawn, born Edwin Meyers Shawn on October 21, 1891, in Kansas City, Missouri. When these two met, married, and formed their school and concert company of Denishawn Dancers, they inadvertently but inevitably became the mother and father of American modern dance. Their "children," Martha Graham, Louis Horst, Doris Humphrey, Pauline Lawrence, and Charles Weidman, became seminal dance figures for succeeding generations.

The lives of St. Denis and Shawn have been explored in many publications. For this book, their influence on American dance may best be comprehended through concentration on their technique, their choreography, their theatrical experiences, the early independent creations of their most noted pupils, and an overview of some recent revivals of their works. To appreciate fully what they contributed to dance culture, certain aspects of their characters should also be examined.

Their backgrounds were curiously similar. Both came from a white, Methodist, middle-class background (hers far more unconventional than his). Both showed a deeply religious instinct early in life that later expressed itself in varied nonsectarian dance forms. Both valued the movement theories of François Delsarte, although each applied those theories in distinctive ways. And both had to make a living as dancers at a time in this country when government and corporate funding for the art of dance was nonexistent.

As personalities, they were alike in ego, ambition, persistence, and charm, but they were not alike in everything. For example, although Miss Ruth hob-nobbed graciously with royalty in Britain, Germany, and the major countries of the Far East, she never became what might be called a sophisticated lady. Shawn, however, seems to have been born sophisticated. They often disagreed about their artistic goals or the practical means to achieve them, and the struggle for professional dominance sometimes threatened their partnership. Yet they never deviated from their deep devotion to dance or to each other, despite the conflicting complications of their long lives together and apart.

They shared the conviction that the art of dance and belief in religion were all-encompassing. Of all the works she choreographed, I believe St. Denis's deepest aim was most closely approximated in those through which she expressed, as its goddesses, the essence of a country: *Radha* (India), *Isis* (Egypt), *Ishtar* (Abyssinia), *Kuan Yin* (China), and *Kwannon* (Japan). Shawn tended to release his spiritual emotions through Christian themes, beginning in 1915 with his *Three Dances of David* (also known as *The Lord Is My Shepherd*). But he, too, found choreographic inspiration in other religions: *A Priest of Gnossos* (also known as *Gnossienne*) and *The Death of the Bull God* (Cretan mythology), *The Invocation to the Thunderbird* (Amerind), *Siva* (Hindu), and *Mevlevi Dervish* and *Ramadan Dance* (Islam). Because these and other works were presented with colorful, original theatricality, the religious strain that persisted throughout the creative lives of St. Denis and Shawn was not always recognized, but those who knew them intimately realized what a sustaining impetus their beliefs remained. In the first issue of the *Denishawn Magazine* (1924) Miss Ruth wrote,

I see a place of magical Beauty, that is and is not of this world we know, a world created of familiar things, but arranged in a new and harmonious order. I see a life lived that bridges the two worlds, the inner and the outer, concept and expression, Nature and Art. I see groves of meditation, where Truth is learned and loved, and halls of Beauty, where the divine self is expressed.

For his part, when Shawn wrote his book *Gods Who Dance,* he quoted Nietzsche's statement, "I should only believe in a God that would know how to dance." He added in his own words, "Many years ago in my first reading of *Thus Spake Zarathustra,* my whole being leaped to ecstatic agreement with this credo. I had already become aware of the fact that no one person can define God, but that each individual had inherited or wrought out his own concept of God."

The last dance St. Denis performed in public was a revival of her East Indian devotional solo *Incense.* The last dance Shawn performed in

Ruth St. Denis in revival of *Radha* as performed at Jacob's Pillow, 1941. Photo, Marcus Blechman. (Collection Suzanne Shelton)

Ted Shawn in *O Brother Sun and Sister Moon: A Study of St. Francis.* Photographed in performance. (Collection Barton Mumaw)

public was his *O Brother Sun and Sister Moon,* a study of St. Francis
that he danced at Jacob's Pillow when he was seventy-five years old. He
called this, "A dance closer to my heart than anything I have ever done."
When together they celebrated their golden wedding anniversary at the
Pillow in 1964, they created their final duet: *Siddhas of the Upper Air* (a
siddha being one who has attained perfection, according to Hindu
belief).

How did this connection between dance and religion happen to come
about in each of their lives? For Ruth St. Denis, it was through her
mother. Ruth Emma Hull Dennis was an ardent early feminist who had
earned a medical diploma. She prescribed for her neighbors medica-
tions and lectures on women's rights in equal doses. A strong-willed
woman who was a dominant figure throughout her famous daughter's
life, she clothed her child in loose dresses or overalls and let her run
barefoot around the farm where they lived. Ruthie had an older step-
brother, a younger brother, and a father who could never adequately
support his brood. Her mother was reduced to running a boarding-
house where she and her daughter made friends with guests who were
Christian Scientists or theosophists.

Her mother also discovered the theories of François Delsarte and
began to teach them to her young hoyden. Delsarte had developed a
"scientific" analysis of body gestures originally intended as a guide for
actors. "To each spiritual function responds a function of the body," he
wrote. "To each grand function of the body corresponds a physical act."
He symbolically divided the body into three areas to demonstrate what
he meant by this: the head represented the mental or spiritual zone, the
upper torso and arms, the emotional zone, and the lower torso and legs,
the physical zone. St. Denis remembered being taught as a child that
"My physical impulses were from the hips down, my emotions were in
the middle of me, and from the shoulders up, all was spiritual."

That free spirit soon made the logical progress from the daily practice
of Delsarte exercises to creating dance stories to taking first formal
lessons in the little town of Somerville, New Jersey, to appearing in that
town's Somerset Hall. Mother Dennis, recognizing talent when she saw
it and audience applause of it, determined that a stage career for her
Ruthie would save the family from poverty. Once she decided this,
nothing swerved the forceful and, it must be admitted, domineering
woman from her goal. By the time Ruth was fifteen, she made her New
York City debut as a "skirt dancer" in Worth's Family Theatre and
Museum. By 1900 she was touring the country in David Belasco pro-

ductions, both as actress and as dancer called on to do anything the script required. (It was this noted playwright, director, and impresario who nicknamed her "Saint Dennis" because of her chaste offstage behavior. It was her mother who not only ensured that behavior but recognized the theatrical value of the nickname.)

When she was about twenty-five years old, St. Denis experienced the two influences that were to shape her life: one a book, the other a picture. During a layoff at home, she began to study her mother's copy of Mary Baker Eddy's *Science and Health with Key to the Scriptures*. Its promise that "All is infinite Mind and its infinite manifestations, for God is All-in-All" became the lodestar of Ruth St. Denis's philosophical convictions. When she again went out on tour that same year, she saw a poster advertising Egyptian Deities Cigarettes with a painting of the goddess Isis. And this became the lodestar of her creative future.

It is well known that she was inspired by this poster to resolve to create a ballet about Egypt. Long before that dream could be realized, however, she won fame in 1906 with her first East Indian dance, *Radha*. Thus began her "goddess syndrome" in forms that exploited everything she and her mother had learned of theatrical artistry in costumes, makeup, and lighting. With this work, along with the religious *Incense* and *Yogi*, the Japanese dance-drama *O-Mika*, and the dramatic solo *The Cobras*, she won acclaim for the next three years, playing opera houses as well as variety halls in England, France, and Germany.

After she returned to the United States, the practical St. Denis realized that her sudden tremendous popularity in vaudeville and at private soirees given by leaders of society did not rest solely on the message of her art. Walter Terry remembers the aging Miss Ruth admitting rue-fully, "I *knew* that all the time I was dancing about God and Faith and the Spirit, most of the audience was only looking at my bare feet and my revealing costume." Yet when she finally did manage to stage her ballet *Egypta* and book a tour for it in 1911, one young man in Denver, seeing her for the first time, was stunned not only by her beauty but by his recognition of what she was trying to say.

That young man was, of course, Ted Shawn. He seems to have inherited a deep religious instinct that established instant empathy with St. Denis's *Isis*. His father had been a successful newspaperman. His mother, to his almost everlasting grief, had died early in his life. She had been related to the Booth family of the noted actors, and even as a small boy Ted wanted to be both a preacher and an actor. When he entered the University of Denver, in which city he and his father were then living, he determined to study for the Methodist ministry. But before he was much older he caught diphtheria. An overdose of the serum prescribed to save his life left him paralyzed from the waist down. Through a combination of will power, therapy, and, no doubt, prayer, he exercised to regain the use of his legs. These exercises led him to dance. (Later, Shawn used to quip that he had danced out of the church into the theatre, while Miss Ruth had started in the theatre and danced into the church.)

His first teacher had once been a ballet dancer at the Metropolitan Opera. His first lessons were therefore in classical ballet, although he was far too old, heavy, and tall, at over six feet, ever to aspire to become a premier danseur. Shawn and his teacher made some money by presenting exhibitions of the varied styles of ballroom dancing that were popular in those days, but ambition drove him to Los Angeles, where he hoped to discover his own way of dancing. While earning his living as a typist, he searched for experienced teachers to help him, yet found none who lived up to his demands. He did, however, find a new partner, Norma Gould, with whom he again began giving exhibitions of the bunny hug, the turkey trot, the one-step, the tango, and the maxixe.

The money he saved from these "tango teas" and from his first attempts at teaching enabled Shawn to quit his stenographer's job. He soon discovered filmed travelogues on exotic lands. These stimulated him to invent more expressive dances than the conventional *Hesitation Waltz* or *French Love Waltz,* which he and Gould had been performing. On their last tour together he programmed a *Grecian Suite* and an *Oriental Suite.* This experience in choreography convinced young Shawn that he needed much more training if ever he was to become the artist he intended to be; he was sure he could find that training only in New York. Once there, by means of teaching and performing, he managed to earn enough to support himself and to take classes in ballet, Spanish dance, and pantomime. Ever since he had seen Ruth St. Denis in *Egypta,* however, he had yearned to study Oriental dance, if possible with St. Denis herself.

In this year of 1914, bookings for St. Denis's rather limited program faced the stiff competition of ballroom dance performances by Irene and Vernon Castle, who were the rage of the day. To meet that competition, Mother Dennis and Ruthie felt that she must have a male partner with whom she could present new works. So it happened that the needs of the comparatively unknown Shawn coincided with the needs of the world-renowned St. Denis. When he appeared to audition for her, Shawn did a dramatic Aztec dagger dance, a pseudo-Grecian "interpretive" number, and a Slavic folk dance. St. Denis immediately accepted him, not, as he had hoped, as a pupil but, to his astonishment, as her partner. That very afternoon they began to talk about their ideas for dance, their personal philosophies, and their spiritual beliefs. It was a conversation they were to continue, with interruptions, until Ruth St. Denis died fifty-four years later.

St. Denis immediately scheduled a tour of the southeastern area of the United States, where her concerts had not previously been seen. In addition to her famous solos, the program included several of Shawn's works. Billed as "Ruth St. Denis, assisted by Ted Shawn, with Hilda Beyer" (his then partner), the three performed at Ravinia Park outside Chicago, then headed south. From this first joint tour until Shawn succeeded in his demand for equal billing in 1921, the name and figure featured on all posters and advertising remained Ruth St. Denis's.

On August 13, 1914, despite the vehement objections of Mother Dennis, the thirty-six-year-old, virginal, famous St. Denis married the twenty-three-year-old neophyte Shawn. Although they were madly in love with each other, they did not permit a long honeymoon to interrupt their dance plans. On August 19 the newlyweds embarked with a small company on a tour that carried them from Saratoga, New York, to San Francisco, where they arrived the following March. With them, as stage manager and sometime dancer, went "René" St. Denis, Ruthie's younger sibling who had never been given any name except Brother, nicknamed Buzz. Their program included some of the best-known St. Denis solos, Shawn's *Dagger Dance,* a selection of the latest ballroom dances performed by Shawn with Hilda Beyer (and by Brother St. Denis with a woman named Alice Martin), and the first duet St. Denis ever danced with her husband. This was part of an *Arabic Suite,* which he had choreographed to music by Rubinstein and Victor Herbert.

The name that was forever to establish them in dance history was not coined until February 6, 1915. An enterprising theatre manager in Portland, Oregon, offered a prize of eight box seats to the person who submitted the best title for a new ballroom exhibition dance St. Denis and Shawn were to perform. When all the contest entries had been judged, the unchallenged winner was "The Denishawn Rose Mazurka." The name Denishawn attracted much publicity and became so popular that it was not long before the St. Denis-Shawn company members became known as the Denishawn Dancers.

In working with these young dancers, St. Denis and Shawn found themselves in agreement with the theories of Delsarte and incorporated

them into their new choreography. Shawn, ever the more intellectual of
the two, delved deeply into Delsarte's writings as he sought to apply his
ideas to Denishawn technique and creations. Eventually, he wrote a
comprehensive book on Delsarte, called *Every Little Movement.*

As the new partners began to influence each other's choice of thema-
tic material in choreography, they also found themselves in agreement
on its religious elements. Among the early solos Shawn created after his
marriage was an entire *Church Service in Dance Form.* In 1920 he
choreographed *Les Mystères Dionysiaques,* for himself and twelve
young women. The first ballet St. Denis co-choreographed with Shawn
was the 1915 *Garden of Kama,* about the Hindu god of Love. This was
followed in 1919 by her incomparable solo representing the Chinese
Goddess of Mercy, *Kuan Yin,* based on studies St. Denis had made of
the bodhisattvas in the Boston and London museums, and danced to
music by Satie.

(It may be appropriate to interrupt here with an explanation of the
word "ballet" as used by Denishawn. Theirs resembled classic ballets in
the sense that they had a story and were full-company productions, with

Ruth St. Denis as Ishtar in her Abyssinian ballet *Ishtar of the Seven Gates.*
Photo, White. (Collection Jane Sherman)

costumes, sets, and special lighting. None of the dancing was done en pointe, however; in partnering, their pas de deux never included lifts; and they did not follow a classic format in the sequence of solos, duos, or ensemble numbers throughout a work. The word ballet is used in this book as it was on Denishawn programs, for lack of a more accurate term with which to categorize *Ishtar of the Seven Gates, Xochitl, The Feather of the Dawn,* or the many other large-scale dance-dramas for which Denishawn was noted.)

Shawn, the born teacher and organizer, soon convinced St. Denis that they should establish a school. To reach agreement on the philosophy that would provide its pedagogical foundation, they had first to spend many hours in deep thought and heart-to-heart discussions. Also, they had to determine the means whereby a teaching institution could be supported. It was Shawn who foresaw sufficient money coming in from their concert tours to finance a school until it could earn its own way. It was St. Denis who originally expressed the aim of what was to become the Denishawn School as "The eternal quest for truth, the ecstasy of an instant's communication with a divine being, the harmony of rituals, beautifully performed."

With the opening in Los Angeles in the summer of 1915 of the Ruth St. Denis School of Dancing and Its Related Arts, the labor to achieve this ambitious goal began.

Chapter Two
The Technique of Denishawn

By 1916 THE SCHOOL formally and officially became known as The Denishawn School. It was intended to fulfill two purposes: to pass on the founders' ideas of a new kind of dance and, eventually, to be a source of steady income. But before St. Denis and Shawn could evolve a definite technique or curriculum, they had to determine essential principles. They finally formulated a guide both for their pedagogy and their choreography:

The art of the dance is too big to be encompassed by any one system. On the contrary, the dance includes all systems or schools of dance. Every way that any human being of any race or nationality, at any period of human history, has moved rhythmically to express himself, belongs to the dance. We endeavor to recognize and use all contributions of the past to the dance and will continue to use all new contributions in the future.

That this was a most ambitious premise on which to found a dance school in those days I can affirm from my own experiences at about the same time. Encouraged by my mother's playing of Red Seal classical music records on our hand-wound Victrola, I had been "dancing" since I was four or five. When we moved to Chicago, I was placed in my first dancing school. There a roomful of children hopped and skipped, curtsied, and turned on their tippy-toes for a few weeks, to be rewarded by appearing in a pupil recital. There I made my debut *(sic)* as one of many butterflies. When the family settled in New York City, I attended "interpretive dance" classes given by a gentle, grey-haired lady whose name I have mercifully forgotten. Her school was in the basement of a church. She required her pupils to wear Grecian dresses made of white cheesecloth, which hung from our skinny shoulders over our long-legged, long-sleeved, baggy winter underwear. At the average age level of ten, we were urged to interpret the music of Ethelbert Nevin and Fritz Kreisler, played on a tinny upright piano by another gentle grey-haired lady as we leaped in our bare feet over the freezing cement floor. Such aimless lack of guidance soon forced me into the hands of a ballet teacher, who shall also be nameless but never forgotten. Before I knew first position from fifth or a plié from a pas de basque, I was put into brand new toe-shoes and encouraged to galumph about the studio with other equally untrained little girls. When I could no longer endure the pain in my aching toes or the sight of my awkward self in the mirror, I struck. No more ballet for me. Only by sheer good fortune did I find Denishawn in 1923.

Such was the general state of affairs in serious dancing schools around the country when, in 1916, Martha Graham discovered Deni-shawn in Los Angeles. She had just graduated from the Cumnock School of Expression shortly after her twenty-second birthday, and her spirit must have found release in the beauty and freedom that St. Denis and Shawn provided their pupils. Their school was housed in a Spanish-type mansion surrounded by eucalyptus trees, on the top of a hill. There was an indoor studio where St. Denis taught some of her classes, and an outdoor platform she used as a site for yoga meditations

Early Denishawn pupils in the Los Angeles School. (Collection Jane Sherman)

and Shawn used for his classes of ballet, ballroom dance, and what was eventually to develop into Denishawn technique.

Miss Ruth did not want the small, rather overweight, and overage Graham as a pupil, so it was on this platform under Shawn's tutelage that Martha began her classes each morning. Before lunch, the students swam in the estate pool, then ate their simple meal at outdoor tables. The grounds have been described as harboring peacocks, but I suspect these birds multiplied in retelling from the single live peacock Ted Shawn gave Ruth St. Denis on their wedding anniversary in 1915. The gift was intended to celebrate not only their first year of marriage but the success of a new dance by St. Denis that had recently won acclaim, *The Legend of the Peacock*. One day this exotic creature literally flew the coop, vanishing into the sky above the school grounds, with Shawn in hot pursuit through the streets of the city until he finally captured the struggling bird and brought it back to its sanctuary.

The students who had attended the first year of the school used to drop the fee of one dollar into a cigar box after each lesson. But to benefit from the publicity of a very profitable vaudeville tour, St. Denis and Shawn decided to charge a fee of $500 for a twelve-week summer course the following year. This course included room and board, two hours of arts and crafts such as tie-dyeing fabrics, five hours of guided reading, two private lessons with St. Denis, and Shawn's daily classes in technique.

These classes lasted for three hours every morning. They began when Shawn led pupils in stretching, breathing, and limbering exercises, then proceeded to ballet barre and floor formations, and from them to the free movement that was to crystallize into the Denishawn style. Miss Ruth would take over with a talk on her belief in the good, the true, and the beautiful, followed by instructions in her own kind of Oriental and yoga techniques.

To this school in 1917 came Doris Humphrey from her own Illinois school. She was a slim, prim person with her auburn hair worn in a high pompadour, and St. Denis was immediately attracted by her personality and her talent. In that same year came Pauline Lawrence, only seventeen years old and just graduated from Hollywood High School, where she had played the piano for class theatrical productions. Dark-eyed, dark-haired, and plump, she wanted to be a dancer, but St. Denis and Shawn valued her ability as an accompanist, so it was as rehearsal and pit pianist, and only as a sometime dancer, in the future, that she joined the Denishawn Company in 1917. She first played for Humphrey

Ruth St. Denis Concert Dancers at the Greek Theatre, Berkeley, Calif. 1920.
Doris Humphrey in center. (Collection Jane Sherman)

during a tour of the Ruth St. Denis Concert Dancers in 1919 to 1920,
when the St. Denis-Humphrey music visualization *Soaring* had its
premiere at the Spreckels Theatre in San Diego, California, on September 9, 1920. She accompanied Graham and Charles Weidman (who
had entered Denishawn in 1919) during the vaudeville tour of Shawn's
ballet *Xochitl* in 1921.

When Shawn came out of the army in 1918, St. Denis was on tour and
the school was closed. He kept one small house in which, with a pianist,
Graham taught some classes. Until 1921 he and St. Denis appeared
together in concert only once, as she sent out her own troupe and he
maintained the school, wrote his book of tribute, *Ruth St. Denis:
Pioneer and Prophet,* and choreographed acts for vaudeville groups and
soloists. In 1920 he opened the Ted Shawn Studio at 932 South Grand
Avenue, featuring Denishawn Dance Productions.

This building became well-known in Los Angeles for its all-black
interiors. The entrance hall had its black walls adorned with Egyptian
designs, and the drawing-room's floors and walls were black, the furni-
ture white. The school's 1921–1922 catalogue announced that "Miss
St. Denis will re-enter teaching work at Denishawn this Fall in preparation for the organizing and building of the Greater Denishawn, while
Mr. Shawn is touring the country in concert. . . . In the summer of 1922,

either Miss St. Denis or Mr. Shawn, or both, will be in the school for the regular Summer course. . . ."

From the beginning, as St. Denis was later to write in her autobiography, "The outline and organization of the Denishawn school was Ted's. My part was to supply, in the unfolding years, the color of the Orient, certain concepts of Music Visualization inspired and derived from Isadora's attitude toward music and dance, and such spiritual inspiration and teaching as could be given within the close and harried activities of a school of the dance." She added, "I don't believe there would ever have been a Denishawn without Ted."

To be sure, Miss Ruth felt that as a creative artist she did not make a good teacher, but she boasted, "I can *inspire* like hell!" And inspire she certainly did when she explained to a class her understanding of East Indian dancing, or her idea of what she called music visualization. This was, as St. Denis defined it, "an abstract concept that related the mechanical structure of movement to the values of music, without reliance upon a dramatic story or a display of technical virtuosity just for its own sake." To be sure, Ted Shawn's basic ballet was adapted to the bare feet on which Denishawn dance philosophy stood, giving the classic steps perforce a softness that might offend purists. Nevertheless, between them this pair of innovators did develop a demanding technique that they taught widely.

As critic Don McDonagh wrote in the *New York Times*, "Denishawn was the first systematic and sustained attempt to provide in Western theatre dance a substantial alternative to ballet. It was also the first to find a means of passing the discipline to others." Martha Graham emphasized in a 1973 interview on WBAI-FM, that "My Denishawn training was rigid. We learned all kinds of ethnic techniques as well as classical ballet as our base, although not, of course, en pointe."

Yet some current writers have perpetuated the fable that St. Denis, Shawn, and the members of their company had no technique. To refute this misconception, consider the fact that from 1915 to 1931 the Denishawn repertory included more than three hundred solos, trios, duos, and group works, as well as sixteen major ballets, programs of which were received with public and critical acclaim in the United States, in every major country of the Orient, in Canada, Cuba, England, and Germany. Denishawn did not achieve this astounding record merely by hopping, skipping, or otherwise tripping the light fantastic through a sea of scarves and a whirlpool of nautch skirts. Had such mindless triviality really formed the technical basis of their performance and choreographic accomplishments, I am certain that St. Denis and Shawn would have long since been forgotten, and their influence on the first generation of modern American dancers would have been nil. It is therefore high time to puncture the myth and recognize the reality.

In my personal experience as a pupil in the New York West 28th Street school of the 1920s there was little contact with Miss Ruth as a teacher. Even later, as an advanced student in the famous Studio 61 at Carnegie Hall, I saw her only when she dropped in unexpectedly to observe a class, or when—like a tall goddess dressed in flowing chiffon—she appeared to talk to us about her ideas of life and dance. I particularly remember two of the thoughts she shared with the adoring girls in their black suits, who sat at her feet like novice nuns before a statue of the Madonna. She told us earnestly, "One should *think* of dance as an art, although one may have to *do* it as a business." She then added in a sober tone of voice, "A talented girl is the result of a mother who has been repressed and into whom goes all that mother's ambition and culture." In rereading my notes much later, I realized that these observations summed up two of the several fundamental conflicts of her life.

All her life, St. Denis was plagued by the need to earn money, not only to live but, far more importantly to her, to realize her vision of what she wanted her dance to say. She and Shawn had many bitter quarrels about when they could not simply think of dance as an art but had to "do it as a business." This continuing difference between them became one of the basic causes for their later separation.

As for Mother Dennis, one cannot claim to know exactly to what degree the frustration she suffered in her medical career found an outlet in her daughter's theatrical career. But there is no doubt that she provided Ruthie with a rich cultural background and was deeply am-bitious for her success. To achieve that aim, Ruth Emma Hull Dennis contributed her own repressed creative ideas, her energy, and her mana-gerial enterprise. She traveled with St. Denis everywhere as companion, counselor, and particularly as chaperone, believing there was no room in her daughter's life for both a man and her art. So strong was the mother's dominance that even when St. Denis reached the age of thirty-six and wished to marry Ted Shawn, she did everything possible to break up the romance. Shawn has written that his final interview with Mrs. Dennis lasted six hours, during which she "raged, ridiculed, appealed to my common sense, turned pathetic, whimpered and laughed through a dramatic performance of enviable range." She capitulated only when faced with St. Denis's unshakable determination to marry Shawn, saying, prophetically, "Ruthie, I still do not think that marriage is wise for you, but I respect your young man, so if you must, marry him. But I warn you, he's no weakling."

The Denishawn School developed into a profitable business. Hundreds of dance teachers from all over the country received their training there, returning home to their own schools to teach Denishawn technique to hundreds of little girls. Since their parents had admired St. Denis and Shawn in concert or vaudeville, they sent their daughters (and a very few sons) to Denishawn as if to a finishing school. They did this with perfect confidence because, as Agnes de Mille once pointed out, "Ruth and Ted were respectable. They were respectable because they were married."

As married couples will, they divided the work. She supplied the glamor and inspiration, he the organization and teaching drive. All their lives, however, both remained omnivorous readers of books on the dance, world cultures, metaphysics, and philosophy, and they shared their enthusiasm for the written word in discussions with their pupils and company members as often as time and strength would permit. The intellectualism that is so impressive in Doris Humphrey's book, *The Art of Making Dances* and in Martha Graham's *Notebooks* can surely be traced back at least in part to the stimulation they had received from these discussions.

At the time when I became a Denishawn pupil at age fourteen, beginners were taught by Hazel Krans and Paul Mathis. In the summer, after the company had concluded the season's tour, advanced students took class in the Carnegie Hall studio. There they were taught by Doris Humphrey, Charles Weidman, and Ted Shawn; either Pauline Lawrence or Louis Horst would be at the piano. (Horst had been engaged in 1915 as a temporary pianist for three weeks of a Denishawn vaudeville tour, and remained with St. Denis and Shawn as their musical director for ten years.)

Teachers of other disciplines were frequently engaged: Ronny Johansson and Margharita Wallmann, for example. Johansson was a student of early Swedish and German modern dance who in 1932 opened her own school in Stockholm. After touring Europe, she came to the United States to teach at Denishawn. When she returned home she founded the Swedish Dance Teachers Organization and remained its secretary for many years. Wallmann was an Austrian choreographer and a member of the Ballets Russes until 1929. She studied with Mary

Wigman in Germany and joined her performing company. When Shawn brought her to Denishawn, she was the first Wigman teacher to come to this country. She later became famous as a director of operas, which she staged in many of the great houses of the world, including New York's Metropolitan.

Out-of-town Denishawn teachers (unforgettably the talented, beautiful Braggiotti sisters Berthe, Gloria, and Francesca from their Boston school) also attended these summer Carnegie Hall classes, as did those Denishawn Dancers not on vacation. All of us wore identical one-piece black wool bathing suits that did little to improve whatever figures we had. We were a mixed bag, indeed, but each and every one of us eagerly followed the required pattern Shawn had designed for acquiring Denishawn technique.

A typical Denishawn class began at the barre; first came stretching, petits and grands battements, a series of pliés in the five positions, sixteen measures of grandes rondes de jambes, and thirty-two measures of petites rondes de jambes. These might be followed by slow relévés en arabesque, fast changés, entrechats, and exercises to prepare for fouettés. In short, the works! During all this we were encouraged as if by Maître Petipa himself to keep knees straight and turned out, to hold buttocks firmly tucked in over heels, to maintain spines erect above center of gravity, to round the arms from relaxed shoulders, to arch the feet with toes sharply pointed.

After ballet arm exercises out on the floor, we next worked to perfect our developés en tournant, our attitudes, our renversés, and our grands jetés. Then each pupil danced alone a series of pas de basques: the Denishawn version, the ballet, the Spanish, and the Hungarian. The Denishawn pas de basque was distinguished by arms held high and parallel overhead as the body made an extreme arch sideways toward the leading foot. When Ted Shawn later formed his Men Dancers, a photograph of him in this step became his personal and company trademark, as it is to this day at Jacob's Pillow.

Next usually came a free, open exercise affectionately nicknamed "arms and body," done to the waltz from Tchaikovsky's *Sleeping Beauty*. A forerunner of the technical warmups now used in many modern dance schools, it started with feet placed far apart and pressed flat on the floor. With a slow swinging of the body into ever-increasing circles, came head, shoulder, and torso rolls, the arms sweeping from the floor toward the ceiling. After a relaxed run around the circumference of the studio, we ended in a back fall. To rest, we might then sit down to practice Javanese arm movements, do hand stretches to force our Western fingers backward into some semblance of Cambodian flexibility, attempt the East Indian nautch dancer's side-to-side "cobra" head slide above motionless shoulders, or work on a pantomime assignment for Charles Weidman.

Class always closed with the learning of another part of a dance. Based on the theory that one learns to perform by performing, dance exercises were essential elements in Denishawn training, and some of them were so professionally interesting that they became part of the concert repertory (*Serenata Morisca*, *Invocation to the Thunderbird*, and *Gnossienne*, for example). As Shawn proclaimed, "We gave our students the richest and most varied fare—old, new, domestic, foreign—anything we felt would enlarge their knowledge of dance that had any value." I especially remember a dance called *Tunisienne* designed to acquaint us with the use of those small finger cymbals known as krotali. There were, in addition, a simple nautch to teach us how to stamp out a rhythm with belled anklets and how to make spiral turns while wearing a full circular skirt; a stately solo called *Lady Picking Mulberries* to familiarize us with the flat-footed, pigeon-toed, bent-kneed walk of a Japanese woman in kimono, and with her handling of a fan and a parasol; a Sevillanas for two couples who donned shoes and accompanied the swift, complex figurations with castanets; a sculpture plastique that demanded great control and balance; and an arduous *Spring, Beautiful Spring* to Lincke's music entitled *Frohsinn*, which means "essence of joy."

Shawn has written that he created this work in 1920 "to give pupils a sense of flow from one phrase to another, to test their endurance in executing consecutive phrases without stopping." It was a test of endurance. And it briefly won a place in Shawn's theatre repertory when, during his tour of Germany and Switzerland in 1931, he needed a solo as a filler in his program. Urged by friends who knew the dance, he reluctantly donned a long-sleeved, long-trousered black silk practice outfit and ventured into the lion's den of German modern dance with this exuberant balletic exercise. He received an incredible number of curtain calls leading to an encore and even more curtain calls.

Our lessons were strict and more or less routine, but we pupils nevertheless absorbed from Miss Ruth, Papa Shawn, Doris, and Charles a deep belief in the art of the dance. Consequently, when we attempted the simplest class dance, even the most untalented among us did it with dignity and feeling. This, too, was an important part of acquiring technique. If a girl were fortunate enough to be chosen from among the many students to be one of the few members of the company, her studio intensity was transformed. Through intimate contact with the Denishawn leaders in rehearsals and in performances, she began to acquire the projection that is essential for communication.

Garson Kanin, director of many Broadway productions, has given an illuminating definition of the kind of projection I mean: "It has nothing to do with volume (i.e., of the actor's voice). It has to do with what is going on in a performer's head and heart. Concentration. The audience has got to know what you are thinking and feeling." Doris Humphrey, in talking about projection as part of performing technique, emphasized the need for absolute conviction in whatever one was dancing. She considered that the body tells almost more than anything else what is really felt, so that without conviction there is automatically very little projection. She saw that when students who worked impassively in class were called upon to convey a dramatic moment on stage, they may have danced it very well but it lost its intended impact because they maintained the same expressionless face as in the studio. It may well be that this lack of projection in latter-day Denishawn revivals contributes to the impression that Denishawn had no technique.

The truth is that St. Denis and Shawn were constantly projecting, not only in their performed message of theatre dance as an art, but in their gospel of teaching methods. In a period when Labanotation and other modern forms of dance-writing had not yet been fully developed, Shawn prepared choreographic notes of exercises and dances for teachers who could not travel to study with him. His writing was succinct, corelating movement to measures of music, and using ballet terms where applicable. But for many Denishawn movements there *were* no convenient established labels. With real creative effort, therefore, Shawn had to describe each such step clearly enough to enable teachers and pupils to learn it at long distance. In this, as in many things, he was ahead of his time.

In 1928 Shawn signed a contract with the Ampico player-piano company to provide ten recordings of Denishawn class music, each to be accompanied by his written notes on exercises and certain class dances. In 1930 he wrote similar choreographic notes for six popular Denishawn class and concert dances. G. Schirmer published these with music and photographs demonstrating steps, formations, and costuming. This was advanced dance pedagogy for its day.

The attitude of St. Denis and Shawn toward the use of music for dance was equally advanced. In the early 1920s they wrote in their *Denishawn Magazine:*

The music of the future will have to be divided into two groups, so far as dancers and the dance public is concerned; that which is to be listened to, and that which is to be danced to.

Beautiful, natural and noble movement can never be trained and fixed in art forms and expressed in supreme works of the dance until the musical compositions offer a sympathetic parallel to the capacity of the human body. But until the ideal music of the future is composed for the express purpose of the dance, we must use the best examples of our classic music as a basis from which to advance to newer and finer forms of both music and dance.

True to these progressive convictions, they often commissioned American composers to write for specific works, notably Louis Horst *(The Royal Ballet of Siam* and *Japanese Spear Dance),* Charles Wakefield Cadman *(Green Nautch),* R. S. Stoughton *(The Spirit of the Sea* and *The Vision of the Aissoua),* Eastwood Lane *(Boston Fancy* and *Around the Hall in Texas),* Lily Strickland Anderson *(The Cosmic Dance of Siva),* and Clifford Vaughan *(White Jade* and *A Burmese Yein Pwe).* Shawn later relied heavily on the gifted Jess Meeker to compose for the works he choreographed for himself and the Men Dancers.

No matter how rigorous their performing and creating schedule, the school was never far from their minds. Even during the hardships of the long Orient tour, Shawn did not neglect the Denishawn schools he had left behind. On many a ship voyage between engagements, when the rest of us were enjoying some hard-earned fun and relaxation, Papa's portable typewriter could be heard clicking away in his cabin as he prepared instructions to mail back home from exotic ports like Batavia or Singapore. In addition to outlining these curricula, he wrote a series of articles for *Dance Magazine* on the Far Eastern dances we had seen. These provided basic information on at least twelve distinct ethnic dance techniques, and were later published in his book *Gods Who Dance.*

St. Denis and Shawn took lessons themselves so that they could incorporate what they learned into their choreography and their curricula. Shawn, always fascinated by Americana, studied American Indian dances at first hand, as well as New England contra dances. In 1923 he went to Spain to work with noted teachers in Barcelona and

Seville, and from there to North Africa to observe the dances of that region. In the Far East, often with their company members participating, Miss Ruth and Papa studied with the outstanding artists Koshiro Matsumoto in Japan, Mei-lan Fan in China, U Po Sein in Burma, Pundit Hira Lal in India, and the Devil Dancers in Ceylon.

Since Oriental techniques were greatly influenced by costume, an advertisement for the 1927 summer courses at the Los Angeles school featured Ruth St. Denis in four weeks of "New dances from the Orient, with full costuming and demonstration lectures, two hours of class and one hour of practice, five days a week." Just as costume handling was considered an essential part of Denishawn technique, so, too, was makeup. When new members joined the company, therefore, we were treated to a breathtaking demonstration of the great lady of dance who felt, quite rightly, that makeup was her special province. Wearing bathrobe and slippers, she sat down before a dressing-table covered with pots, pans, powder puffs, and other paraphernalia, and proceeded to make up her own face as she wanted us to learn to do for our music visualization dances. Within an astonishingly few minutes, Miss Ruth transformed herself from a studio mortal into the stage luminary who made viewers weep when she danced her *Liebestraum*. She then showed us how to alter this basic makeup to give our eyes a Chinese or Japanese slant, to tan our complexions a West or East Indian hue, or to shade our cheeks a rosy Spanish glow.

It was this kind of attention to detail that imbued Denishawn productions with the color, the character, and the originality that attracted not only enthusiastic audiences to their concerts, but so many pupils to their schools that in the 1930s and 1940s there was a popular saying around the theatre: "Scratch a dancer and you'll find Denishawn." When one did find Denishawn, one discovered more than two glamorous innovators—more than a company that could perform many different kinds of dances in a single program—more than ethnic creations that could sell out Carnegie Hall for a record-breaking four consecutive performances. One discovered the rich and varied technique without which Ruth St. Denis and Ted Shawn could not have elevated the public's taste from their first two-a-day vaudeville tour together in 1915 to their last Denishawn appearance together at the Lewisohn Stadium in 1931; without which, indeed, they could not have produced that next seminal generation of dancers who in turn (and through *their* descendents) elevated the art of modern dance to a level that is recognized worldwide as a great and distinctly American achievement.

Chapter Three
Some Denishawn Dancers
(1919–1931)

I HAVE OFTEN BEEN asked by dance students what the members of the Denishawn company were like. To answer this as best I can I must draw mainly on my own memories as a Denishawn Dancer and peripherally on the experiences of Denishawn personnel of other years as they were confided to me. Basically, who and what the Denishawn Dancers were was determined by the kind of society in which we then lived, by the character of Ruth St. Denis, and by the availability of talented young men and women dancers.

In my day and before, so far as I have been told, we were what I would call a homogenized group. All were white. Most had had at least a high school education. Most were probably Protestant, but none I knew regularly attended church, nor were any of us interested in querying what the others believed. We were all Americans, from different parts of the country: the Grahams from Santa Barbara, California; Humphrey from Oak Park, Illinois; Weidman from Lincoln, Nebraska; Anne Douglas from Seattle, Washington; Edith James from Phoenix, Arizona, by way of Texas; Ernestine Day from Arkansas City, Kansas; George Steares from Buffalo, New York; Barton Mumaw from Eustis, Florida; myself from Beloit, Wisconsin, and New York City; and so on. Our backgrounds varied from working class to professionals to upper middle-class. As students, we were encouraged by St. Denis and Shawn to explore the metaphysical universe, but few of us questioned the real world in which we lived. This lack of curiosity seemed typical of the young people of the times, and we were also so involved in dance that we did not care much about what was happening beyond the studio or stage door.

Miss Ruth and Papa should not be faulted because they had no Black or Hispanic members in their company. In those days, except for pupils at settlement houses or in ghetto cultural centers, few Blacks and Hispanics had the money or opportunity to study dancing in a prejudiced environment where only the most menial jobs were open to them. Certainly they never came to study at Denishawn. This left only "WASP" dancers from which to select company members, since that selection was almost always made from among the students at the Denishawn Schools.

And how were these choices made? It is my impression that Miss Ruth looked for girls who were slim, pretty (in the conventional sense), and who possessed a spiritual quality; whereas Shawn searched for dancing ability and a personality that would project across the footlights. Sometimes they disagreed, as they had about Martha Graham, who was Shawn's discovery (St. Denis appreciated her gifts only much later). Sometimes they were fortunate to find a Doris Humphrey, an Anne Douglas, a Geordie Graham or an Ernestine Day who incorporated the ideals they both sought. These were the ones who remained with the company for years, unless they themselves chose to leave. Miss Ruth and Papa could not afford to be terribly particular about the male dancers they needed because, as with Blacks and Hispanics, few young men were then studying their kind of serious dance. Despite this, they found Weidman, Robert Gorham, Jack Cole, Barton Mumaw and a handful of other male dancers who demonstrated real theatrical, musical, and technical talents.

Gertrude Shurr (a 1925 Denishawn teacher and later a leading figure in the Martha Graham and May O'Donnell companies and schools) wrote me in reference to my book, *The Drama of Denishawn Dance:* "At last someone has set the record straight as to the sincerity, the structured training, which produced dancers for the all-encompassing techniques Denishawn dances demanded. No dancer today has this varied and cultural knowledge." She went on to reminisce rather wistfully,

I, too, appreciate Mr. Shawn for what he did for dance, although when I studied at Denishawn, it was Miss Ruth, Doris and Charles. *He* was my idol. In the summer of 1927, Miss Ruth choreographed *The Basket Dance* and *The Sacred River* on two of us. Then we would dance them in front of the class as Miss Ruth talked and gestured the movements—as only she could. . . . This was one of the greatest experiences of my dance life. . . . The Chopin Nocturne was the dance

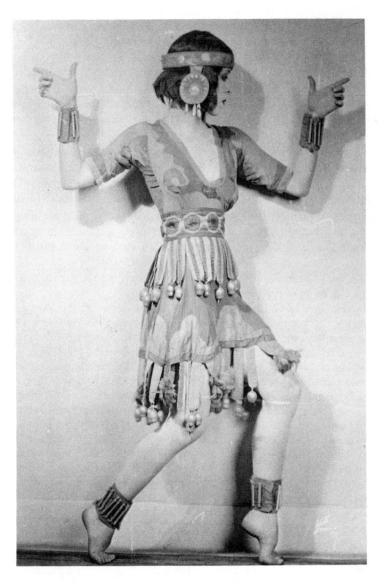

Martha Graham in *Xochitl*, 1923. Photo courtesy of the Dance Collection, New York Public Library.

Mr. Shawn did that summer. Pauline Lawrence and I would get to the studio by 8:30 A.M., and Mr. Shawn worked on the dance and I wrote notes as he did this, and then he would teach what he had created in the morning, to the advanced class. This, too, was exciting.

In a later letter, she wrote me, "I am glad you are so clear-headed. I never heard Doris, Martha or Charles say anything about Mr. Shawn. It was only about Miss Ruth and in terms of respect and a kind of awe. This they instilled in me, too. Their feelings about Mr. Shawn were never revealed to any of us. . . ."

As might be expected, the company members had different attitudes toward their leaders. No doubt the reactions I have received from some of the few Denishawn Dancers who still survive come from the hindsight of years, but there remains sufficient immediacy in their reporting of their experiences to give credence to their feelings about St. Denis and Shawn.

Anne Douglas, a company member from 1919 to 1927, wrote me:

People had such different experiences with Miss Ruth and Mr. Shawn, how can it all add up to one impression? I was not a dedicated dancer, as Charles [Weidman] used to say about dancers. For me it was a wonderful way to earn my living. . . . You [Jane] started at about the same age I did but with such a different contact with Miss Ruth and Mr. Shawn. I was a replacement for a girl who had left a Denishawn vaudeville act, and I didn't even see them [i.e., St. Denis and Shawn] until much later. . . . After that, at night rehearsals of *Julnar of the Sea*, Mr. Shawn would ask Miss Ruth to see what he was creating. We would do what we had worked on, then I could always see that he was carefully trying to choose the right words, because he never could accept her opinion. We had blue flannel robes and would wrap up in them and lie on the floor away from Miss Ruth and Mr. Shawn, in groups, until the argument was over. I was used to hearing them before I ever knew Miss Ruth at all. . . . The only *personal* conversation I ever did have with Miss Ruth was in Hong Kong in 1926 when, for some reason, I took something to her dressing-room. She suddenly asked me if I were going to marry a man I had met in Singapore. I was so surprised that she thought of me as a person after all those years that I just mumbled 'No' and left!

Geordie Graham, Denishawn Dancer from 1921 to 1928, followed her sister Martha into the school, then quite literally into her footsteps in several dances after Martha left Denishawn, particularly as the lead with Shawn in *Xochitl*. Her own distinctive talent shone brightly in her *Danse Cambodienne* during the 1926–1927 United States tour after

A Scene from *Xochitl,* 1923. In central group: Geordie Graham, Robert Gorham, Ted Shawn, Charles Weidman. On left: Lenore Scheffer, Louise Brooks, Martha Hardy. On right: Theresa Sadowska, Doris Humphrey, Anne Douglas. Photo, White. (Collection Jane Sherman)

the Orient. Geordie especially revered St. Denis because they shared a mystical approach to dance. It was therefore Geordie who wrote me in 1979 how she remembered something I had forgotten or, more likely, had never experienced ". . . the half hour we had to sit in silence before performances was all so tender. The stage was for us a sacred place, and so it has remained for many. I could never get used to the nervousness of the commercial theatre."

The glamorous Louise Brooks, who later became a world-renowned film star (see her *Profile* by Kenneth Tynan in the *New Yorker* for June 6, 1979 and her 1982 book *Lulu in Hollywood*), was a company member from 1922 to 1924. In a letter written to me in 1980 she minced no words about her reactions to Miss Ruth and Papa:

. . . the rule set up by St. Denis and Shawn was never to speak my name or run the Hopi ballet photos of Mr. Shawn and me [after she left the company]. When I got Eastman House [in Rochester, New York, where she then lived] to copy a Shawn ballet for him about twelve years ago [i.e., some time in the 1960s] on the phone I asked Mr. Shawn why I was blacklisted. He was fittingly embarrassed. The truth is that Miss Ruth detested me, and both of them longed to be movie stars. . . . I was a lousy dancer and didn't mind at all when Miss Ruth threw me out.

(Note that she could not have been so "lousy" when throughout two tours of the United States she was assigned many group, trio, and at least two solo dances, as well as the lead with Shawn in *The Feather of the Dawn* Hopi Indian ballet.)

Anna Austin, who was a Denishawn Dancer from the *Ziegfeld Follies* 1927–1928 tour through 1932, toured that last year with Shawn without St. Denis. Her heart was always with Miss Ruth, however, whom she adored and to whom she returned after the Denishawn breakup, to stay as coteacher through many difficult years of devotion.

As for myself, when I joined the company in 1925 at age seventeen to remain a member for three years, I saw Miss Ruth as an immortal being who could do no wrong, and Ted Shawn as the most fantastic dancer on earth. Inevitably, I discovered that neither of them spent their lives on a pedestal, in the theatre or out.

Ted Shawn was the teacher, the "impresario," the rehearsal task-master, but it was Miss Ruth's character, as I have said, that greatly determined the choice of Denishawn Dancers. That character also shaped our behavior. Everyone who ever knew her agreed that she

Finale of the ballet *Feather of the Dawn*. Louise Brooks, Ted Shawn, and members of the 1923–1924 Denishawn Company. Photo, White. (Collection Jane Sherman)

could be a dazzling goddess at one moment, then at the very next an untidy companion giggling at gossip over a cup of tea. St. Denis was never a snob. She held her head with its prematurely white hair high in the clouds of her aspirations, but she kept her rather pigeon-toed feet firmly on the ground of day-to-day life. She was notoriously idealistic, yet she also had a caustic, sometimes cruel, wit. She loved hearing and telling a good joke. She endured with patience and fortitude the strains of touring in an era when there were none of the conveniences and comforts we consider essential today.

For instance, we crossed the Pacific Ocean by ship when there was no air travel or air mail, and played through the intolerable heat of the Far East when there was no air-conditioning. At home or abroad, we had no television or portable radios; no permanent waves, bobby pins, or hair dryers; no Kleenex, Kotex, Tampax, or nail polish; no nylon pantyhose, no wash'n'wear synthetic materials, no zippers; no bandaids, vitamins, tranquilizers, penicillin, reducing pills, cold pills, or—needless to say—birth control pills. (These would not have been necessary in any case, however, because all female Denishawners were unmarried and, presumably, virginal.)

As did Miss Ruth and Papa Shawn, we endured these working conditions because we had been inspired to believe in dance as a great art form. Also, Denishawn was then the only dance company that paid for such long tours that its members could almost earn a year-round salary. This, for the novice, was forty dollars a week, from which we had to pay for hotel, food, makeup, and personal needs, but not, fortunately, for transportation. For each additional year a member stayed with the company, she or he received a five-dollar-a-week raise. As Gertrude Shurr noted, "You really lived and performed under circumstances that would make a union cry 'Slave labor!'"

St. Denis and Shawn lived under similar financial circumstances. Although they often earned large amounts from their tours, they had to spend those dollars so swiftly on new productions that they were never free from worry about money. As Shawn was to say when he was an old man, "I have been burdened all the time with the simple fight for survival." It was not until their performing days were long over that the kind of help available for dance today came into existence: college residencies, public support, corporate and government grants were unheard of.

When he was seventy-nine years old, Shawn once said to Barton Mumaw,

"Do you know how much help some of the other dancers get? Why, one year, I think it was when I was seventy-five, Martha Graham not only got the $35,000 Aspen Award but a Federal grant for $181,000! Limón received $23,000. Anna Sokolow $10,000. Antony Tudor $10,000, and Ailey, Cunningham, Alwin Nikolais, and Paul Taylor $5,000 apiece.

"I don't begrudge them this, you know. But wouldn't you think by now that I have struggled enough so that a grant would not weaken my moral fibre? Or maybe," he joked with a pained smile, "maybe like body odor or halitosis, I emit something that repels money, heh?"

Despite often formidable financial difficulties, however, Shawn always appeared the perfect gentleman in public, resembling a successful stock broker more than a struggling dancer. Miss Ruth always tried to appear the perfect gentlewoman because she was resolved to disprove the cliché that all dancers lived the unconventional life of an Isadora Duncan, a resolve she instilled in her "children." We were to deport ourselves like the well-brought-up little girls she wanted us to be. We were expected to wear hats and stockings at all times offstage, and in all climates. No matter how weary or woebegone, we gamely had to don evening dresses for command appearances at after-performance supper parties.

Even in the privacy of our theatre dressing-rooms, Miss Ruth insisted we wear pink cotton underpanties. Even in the south of India or the heart of Java where the temperature, with unbearable humidity, frequently reached 110 degrees, she might suddenly pop through our door to see if we were all decently pantied. Onstage, female dancers always had to wear white body paint, the males brown. (This promptly melted away in droplets of perspiration during the first ten minutes of dancing, but no matter.) Furthermore, no Denishawn Dancer was allowed to smoke, to drink, or, if she were a young woman, to accept a date with a man unless she was chaperoned. I admit we sometimes got around that regulation without Miss Ruth's seeming knowledge. But drink or smoke? Never.

I do not know when or why another Denishawn tradition was established but it was fully entrenched by the time I became a company member and it may well have arisen from necessity: all Denishawn Dancers were responsible for the day-to-day care of their own costumes and wigs. Since St. Denis and Shawn often took several completely different programs on a long tour, this could mean as many as twenty or more numbers for which we had to iron all varieties of costumes, and dress with coconut oil, brush, comb, and pins the hairpieces of various styles. Pearl Wheeler, Denishawn's fabulous costume designer and Miss Ruth's personal friend and dresser, repaired any major wear and tear. But woe betide the dancer who failed to launder her silk, flesh-colored basic leotards nightly, or who carelessly pressed the yards of tiered ruffles on a Spanish skirt. And heaven help the one who gained a few pounds to strain the seams of the costumes that had been specially made to fit her original figure. Furthermore, because each program listed numbers that demanded we portray different characters, we had to be adept at quick changes, not only of costume and wig but of makeup, applied, as Miss Ruth had taught us, to suit all our ethnic as well as our non-ethnic dances.

The procedure before each new performance was automatic. As soon as our floorcloth was laid over the theatre stage, our cyclorama hung, and our sets and lighting equipment were unloaded, our costume trunks, each marked with the distinctive blue-and-yellow Denishawn stripes, were delivered from train or ship. In the ordinary course of events, we dancers arrived in the afternoon, located the trunks in the basement of the theatre, did our ironing, hung our costumes in the dressing-rooms assigned us, dressed our wigs, and laid out our makeup. Then we had a brief rest at the hotel, if there were time, and a light supper.

This was the routine we followed whether we were appearing at the extraordinarily modern Imperial Theatre in Tokyo, with its spotless, straw-matted dressing-rooms and its enormous Japanese-style bath on every floor, or in a bare Texas arena that still bore distinct signs of the horse show that had immediately preceded us. We grew hardened to filthy backstage conditions, to small town hotel rooms that reeked of the cigar stubs left behind by traveling salesmen, to the practically inedible food of all-night beaneries. Except when in the Orient we had had the luxury of long sea voyages between engagements, travel was exhausting. To make most one-night stand jumps we had to catch trains at dawn, sleep as best we could on our coach seats of cindery wool or straw, and, on arrival at our destination, make a beeline to hotel and theatre.

It was a rugged, uninspiring life that required great stamina and optimism. These were rewarded at every performance, however, when in our makeup and freshly pressed costumes, under lighting that transformed each weary one of us into a beauty, we heard the notes from the piano that marked our first entrance of the evening. Show after show for years, in every nook and cranny of the country, St. Denis and Shawn, Humphrey and Weidman had endured that life yet responded to their inspiration without letdown. The rest of us felt that the least we could do was follow their example.

Onstage, Shawn exerted tremendous magnetism and St. Denis projected unequaled presence and charm. Her involvement in the message of her dances seemed absolute. She had such a drive for perfection, however, that even as she performed a solo for the umpteenth time on the umpteenth tour, she kept a sharp eye on everything happening around her. I fell victim to that sharp eye when I made my first appearance in the ensemble of the Spanish ballet *Cuadro Flamenco*. After I had changed into my black wig, I remembered Miss Ruth's earlier instructions to add more rouge to my basic makeup whenever dark hair was called for. Garbed in my Spanish costume, I was happily clapping and shouting "Olé!" for the big St. Denis solo when, in the middle of a renversé turn that displayed her remarkable backbend, she stopped dead to stare at me. On the next turn, she called out of the corner of a smile, "You look like a clown!" On the final turn, with its flurry of heel-beats, she commanded, "See me in my dressing-room!" Mortified, not knowing what to expect, I reported there in fear and trembling right after the show. Miss Ruth kindly but firmly sat me at her dressing-table to give me a lesson in makeup as she toned down my far too-scarlet cheeks.

As one who watched her through some seven hundred performances during my years as a Denishawn Dancer, I can say that out of boredom or absent-mindedness St. Denis frequently changed steps here and there in the solos she had danced hundreds of times. She and Shawn were so dedicated, however, that they unfailingly gave every audience everything it expected to see, no matter how dispirited or distracted they might have been. As for the company, we seldom had an opportunity to warm up before a concert, few rehearsals were held once a number had been set, and we knew neither Miss Ruth nor Papa rarely watched us from the wings so they might criticize or compliment our work. They knew they could rely on us to do our best.

As long as I was with them, I do not recall either one of them ever canceling an appearance or missing a dance because of illness. Miss Ruth, especially, seemed blessed with the sturdy physique inherited from her New Jersey farm childhood that enabled her to live an active life for eighty-nine years. The key to her energy, to her wicked sense of fun, her earthiness beneath the ethereal exterior, might indeed be found in the paraphrase of an old saying: You can take the artist out of New Jersey but you can't take New Jersey out of the artist.

As that artist, and as head of a company of young people who looked to her for guidance, St. Denis evinced not the least maternal feeling. Except in isolated instances, for most of her Denishawn Dancers she remained the aloof Miss Ruth. Undoubtedly it was her remoteness that led us to take our personal troubles to Ted Shawn who, although closer to us in years, had a recognizably warm, fatherly side to his character. Perhaps this is why a fifteen-year-old pupil at one of the earliest California schools had nicknamed her teacher "Papa" and why Denishawners affectionately called him that ever after.

Chapter Four
Some Denishawn Dances
(1906–1931)

OF THE ERA WHEN Denishawn began, Ted Shawn was quoted in his obituary in the *New York Times,* January 10, 1972, as having said "The only ballet was at the Metropolitan Opera and it was so bad you wouldn't believe it. Dancers in musicals kicked sixteen to the right, sixteen to the left, and kicked the backs of their heads. In vaudeville you had the soft shoe, the sand shuffle and the buck and wing." He might well have added to this dismal picture that American audiences had rare opportunities to see authentic ethnic dance of any kind, including their own Amerind, and that after the final appearances of Isadora Duncan on the stages of New York and Boston, only limited examples of the free barefoot dancing for which she was famous. It was Denishawn that ventured into the hinterland of our country to perform in colleges, concert halls, vaudeville theatres, convention centers, and outdoor stadiums their versions of Oriental, Spanish, American Indian, and what was then called Grecian interpretive dancing.

In no instance did St. Denis or Shawn assert that these versions were reproductions of the real thing. They were not supposed to be. Denishawn "translations" were presented with theatrical color and know-how, with costumes and makeup that approximated the authentic, and with music chosen for a proper flavor. St. Denis and Shawn were honorable in intent and respectful of details as they offered wide audiences glimpses of cultures they had never before experienced. In preparing every new ethnic work, the two immersed themselves in studies of the books, paintings, sculpture, and music of that area, even to discovering in a museum a tiny, ancient coin that showed the correct headdress for St. Denis to wear in her Abyssinian ballet, *Ishtar of the Seven Gates.*

Whenever possible, as in Spain, Cuba, and the Far East, both leaders studied with dance teachers in those countries. Their difficult aim was always by this means to recapture the spirit of the culture rather than to reproduce in a mechanical way steps that were easily learned. It was the re-creation of that spirit that made Denishawn's contribution to dance unique.

In the following examples of St. Denis and Shawn works that I have chosen to describe, I have arbitrarily, but I think logically placed them in four categories: Orientalia, Americana, Music Visualization, and Miscellanea.

Orientalia

It is appropriate to begin with Oriental works because chronologically and choreographically these demonstrate the impetus that launched Denishawn. They were almost exclusively the province of St. Denis. Shawn created comparatively few outstanding Oriental solos and group numbers, although he played essential roles in Egyptian, Siamese, Japanese, and Abyssinian ballets. Martha Graham, while she was with the company from 1921 through 1923, danced some minor Far Eastern solos, trios, and ensembles. Charles Weidman appeared in the major Oriental ballets and a few lesser works. Doris Humphrey similarly appeared in those ballets and one or two small ensemble dances, but *Serenata Morisca* and her leading role in *A Burmese Yein Pwe* were the only Oriental solos I can recall her doing.

St. Denis's *Radha* (as first seen at the New York Theatre on January 28, 1906, subtitled *The Mystic Dance of the Five Senses*) was the spark that started a revolution in the art of American serious theatrical dance. To music from Delibes's *Lakmé*, it was a mini-ballet built around a series of solos set in a Hindu temple with a background ensemble of priests. Throughout, an exotic brown-painted and barefooted young woman moved with sinuous arms, rippling fingers, belled anklets, spiral turns that flared her gauzy skirt into scallops of golden hem, and deep backbends that displayed her supple waist.

At the opening, Radha is seen sitting motionless in her shrine in the lotus position, under a spotlight of changing colors. When she ceases her prayers, she rises to begin "The Dance of Sight," during which she manipulates ropes of pearls. She next does "The Dance of Hearing" to the rhythms of loops of bells. For "The Dance of Smell" she moves voluptuously with a garland of marigolds, to end with a sensuous

Doris Humphrey in *Serenata Morisca*. This is the only known solo that both Humphrey and Martha Graham performed in public during their days with Denishawn. Photographed in performance at the Imperial Theatre, Tokyo, 1925. (Collection Jane Sherman)

gesture when she crushes the flowers to her face and body. Next, picking up a bowl for "The Dance of Taste," she mimes drinking that climaxes into intoxication when she sinks to the floor. There, kneeling in the center of her circular skirt, she performs "The Dance of Touch" through movements with which she caresses her hands, arms, torso, and throat. With a crescendo of the music she rises in "The Delirium of the Senses," which ends in swift spins until she suddenly falls to the stage as the lights go down. When they come up again, we see the goddess kneeling for "The Renunciation of the Senses." She stands as the lighting grows brighter, then moves backward toward her shrine where eventually the idol, again lost in meditation, sits in her original pose.

In contrast to this creation, which for its time was audacious in its frenzied sensuality, St. Denis choreographed *White Jade* twenty years later to music by Clifford Vaughan. This was a dance of stillness that embodied the spirit of another culture. At the Temple of Heaven, St. Denis had sensed standing before her under the grey skies of Peking, a vision of the Chinese Goddess of Mercy. Drawing inspiration from her earlier solo *Kuan Yin*, she created a quiet, devout representation of that figure entirely in white. As in *Radha*, she is discovered sitting onstage,

Ruth St. Denis in *White Jade*. (Collection Jane Sherman)

but now on a low, red lacquer platform placed against a tall screen of dull gold and illuminated by a blueish white light. From the crown of her pearl and chiffon headdress to her white face (with only the eyes and mouth touched with color) to her long, whitened hands to the folds of the robe of weighted white chiffon that flows around her, she is the personification of all the porcelain and milky jade figures of Kuan Yin that she had so meticulously studied. When she slowly rises to leave the platform, her feet are hidden by the costume so that she appears to glide from one stately yet gentle pose to another. Two large white porcelain vases containing white lotus flowers flank the platform. She approaches the first to raise a small white bottle that holds the Water of Life, which she pours down her draperies as she inclines her body graciously, sedately, to the right. She then glides to the opposite side where she lifts a white porcelain basket that contains a fish representing Health and Fertility. Moving thus from one perfect pose to another, she eventually returns to the platform. There she resumes her original sitting posture with her right hand resting on her slightly upraised right knee and, as the lights fade, she lowers her eyes.

Presenting another aspect of the Far East, Shawn's 1919 *Japanese Spear Dance* to music especially composed by Louis Horst explored the tradition of combining athleticism with artistry. Although he had yet to visit Japan to see the real thing, Shawn's imagined samurai fighting an imagined enemy came amazingly close to being authentic. His facial makeup, wig, and costume had been copied from Japanese prints, but he had to rely upon his own creativity to impersonate the menacing, powerful, graceful warrior manipulating a six-foot-long spear with a curved blade of actual steel. He builds a little drama around the search for his foe, their confrontation, his own wounding, disarming, and consequent recovery of his fallen spear. Throughout the dance, he grunts and hisses and mutters pseudo-Japanese imprecations to lend credibility to the swift, violent action. He ends his solo in a terrifying spin at stage center, holding the spear straight out in his right hand parallel to the floor, occasionally lowering the weapon to leap over it. Then he abruptly assumes a pose of victory as he faces the audience with both his knees bent outward in deep pliés, jabbing the handle of the spear at arm's length to the right, his head poised arrogantly as the lights black out. In 1926 a Calcutta critic wrote of this dance that ". . . the expressive pantomime of combat found exactly appropriate interpretation in movements of rare abstract beauty." The solo remained in Shawn's Denishawn repertory until the last company performances of

1931–1932. It reappeared on the program of the famous first all-male modern dance concert in Boston in 1933, and was programmed on subsequent concerts of the Men Dancers on tour until 1939.

When in 1919 St. Denis came down to earth from her East Indian goddesses to portray a slightly venal nautch dancer, it is hard to conceive of any audience that could resist her *Green Nautch,* probably the most popular dance in her large repertory. In the green satin, wide-gold-bordered circular skirt from which the solo got its name, she was allure itself as she looked out into the theatre from beneath a gold-colored and gold-braid-banded silk chuddar (headsheet).

To music by Charles Wakefield Cadman, she enters illuminated by a bright spotlight against a black velvet backdrop. Her slow, casual, hip-swinging walk flings the full skirt into voluptuous folds, her anklets tinkle with each step. With a salaam of both her beautiful bejeweled hands to her bejeweled forehead, she greets the audience seductively, with a trace of mockery, before she begins the languid belled-foot stamping that signals the start of the dance. It is a dance that quickly comes to life with turns that spiral from bent knees to highest half-toe, with abrupt hip thrusts to one side then the other, with snakelike arms, and cobra head-slides accented by semaphoring eyebrows. At one point she stops abruptly to hold out a hand toward the front rows and demand "Baksheesh!" After a long spin, body and head arched backward, she suddenly halts, looks out at her viewers with an expression of boredom and contempt, flings her headsheet over one shoulder, and walks offstage.

Of similar earthiness but completely different style was Doris Humphrey's solo in the Burmese ballet, *A Burmese Yein Pwe,* which she and St. Denis choreographed in Singapore in 1926. Long famous for her ethereal *Hoop* and *Scarf* dances, fleet-footed but strong, elfin but serious, Humphrey here surprised audiences by her perfect interpretation of a minx of a Burmese dancer. She was garbed in a costume that seemed to assure immobility: the traditional floor-length tight-fitting, brilliant silk skirt, with a starched white, long-sleeved, sheer muslin bodice. From the top of her black, lacquered, flower-decorated wig to the tips of her bare toes, she was the double of many performers the Denishawn Dancers had watched in Burma at their *yein pwes,* or festivals.

As did these amazingly athletic Burmese dancers, Doris, hobbled from waist to knees, performs swift side jumps, impossible body arches, bent-kneed turns, and low kicks of the feet in a step that resembles the kazatsky. At the same time, from the waist up, her arms and hands are in constant motion of double-jointed flexibility. Everything is done quickly and with exhausting vigor. Yet Humphrey captures the spirit of every tricky contortion she could manage to do. She "smokes" a thick green cheroot, flirts, using two small fans, manipulates a short silk scarf tied around her waist, and culminates her solo in a deep backbend in profile to the audience, all the while furiously twirling a parasol in each hand. (The music was especially composed by Clifford Vaughan.)

As expertly as she performed it, this was not the kind of dancing Doris enjoyed doing and I, for one, was not surprised to learn she had written her mother that ". . . the Burmese is Oriental applesauce." Despite Humphrey's personal success in this difficult impersonation, the Burmese ballet remained in the Denishawn repertory only from its Singapore debut in July 1926, to the end of the Arthur Judson United States tour in 1927.

On the return tour home by way of China and Japan, Shawn first presented what I believe was his greatest Oriental creation, if not one of the greatest of all his solos, *The Cosmic Dance of Siva,* to music he commissioned by Lily Strickland Anderson. It was applauded with enthusiasm at its premiere in Manila in September 1926; it received ovations when Denishawn filled Carnegie Hall in April 1927. Incongruous as it seems, it also invariably stopped the show when he danced it in the *Ziegfeld Follies* for forty weeks, and it continued to be acclaimed through the second Lewisohn Stadium concert of 1928, during Shawn's solo tour of Germany in 1930, and when he last danced it twenty-five years later at Jacob's Pillow.

He wears a coat of brown paint and forty pounds of solid silver belts, bracelets, anklets, and headdress. He confines all movement to three small, graduated platforms placed deep upstage in an eerie lighting that shifts from golden to flame and back again. There he achieves the impossible of performing Siva's dances of Creation, Preservation, Destruction, and Reincarnation. He arches and bends his torso, knees, arms, head, and hands into poses copied from the sculptured walls of ancient Indian temples. He halts for long breathless moments on the high half-toe of one foot. Restricted in floor space as the solo is, it is never static, never lacking in intense involvement. Its opening frozen position, where Shawn balances on his right foot with his left leg held high across his body, changes slowly but logically to frantic stomping, turning, and twisting that represents devastation. Then the god resumes his original pose of spirit incarnate and the dance ends.

Shawn made even *Follies* audiences believe in the other worldly power that had inspired the work and continued to inspire every performance of it. As had Miss Ruth with her Radha, I think Papa's Siva made a significant contribution to Western understanding and acceptance of East Indian art forms.

Americana

St. Denis found her most powerful inspiration in the Far East, and it might be said that Ted Shawn found his in the cultures of the Americas. He maintained a steady interest in American composers even while Louis Horst introduced into Denishawn choreography the works of many of the then avant-garde European musicians. Shawn frequently commissioned or used the compositions of such Americans as Nathaniel Dett, Edward MacDowell, Charles Tomlinson Griffes, Bainbridge Crist, Deems Taylor, Carrie Jacobs Bond, Jess Meeker, and others. He particularly studied and deeply respected Amerind traditions. From his 1917 *Invocation to the Thunderbird* (John Philip Sousa) to his 1921 Aztec ballet *Xochitl* (Homer Grunn) to his 1923 Hopi ballet *The Feather of the Dawn* (Charles Wakefield Cadman), he presented the results of his studies in colorful interpretations that won great praise.

In Berlin, during his 1930 solo tour of Germany, he gave the first performance of his *Osage-Pawnee Dance of Greeting,* a work that represented the meeting of two friendly tribes. Over the years, as sometimes happened at Denishawn, it suffered sea changes from solo to small group to ensemble. It was still being done by four of his Men Dancers as late as 1938. Shawn and/or his dancers wore a chamois cap to imitate a shaved skull bisected by an upright fore-and-aft brush of hair. His body was painted reddish-tan. Two long beaded and fringed buckskin panels hung front and back from a beaded belt, and moccasins were on his feet.

To a tom-tom beat rhythm, the dancer enters upstage with a toe-heel step, body crouched low, hands holding gourds that rattle an accent on each beat. On a high note, he jumps upright, clashing the gourds over his head. There follow formations of hop steps with knees still bent, and formations where the head is flung back, the arms spread high and wide in a gesture of exultation. A shake of the gourds on each subsequent toe-heel step reaches a crescendo when the arms are held out straight forward. After circling the stage and moving through a figure-eight combination of hop steps, the dancer abruptly stops at midstage in semiprofile. The right arm bends upward at the elbow and is held forward, the left elbow bends downward as that arm is held in back. With the body's weight on the left foot, on the last note of music, the right toe sweeps forward to touch the floor, both knees bent, a pose that is held until blackout.

As with the majority of Denishawn ethnic works, Shawn made here no attempt to reproduce an authentic Indian dance, but rather to capture the spirit of the specific tribes he had studied. It is notable that although they were very possessive of their dances, the members of these tribes paid Shawn the rare compliment not only of attending his performances but of delighting in them.

Shawn's fascination with American culture extended beyond the Amerind to New England contra dance, to the barn dances of his Kentucky forebears, to the cowboy, to the Black heritage and the Hispanic influence, to the sports world, and to his observations of particular aspects of American character. In 1923, he had been quick to capitalize on Charles Weidman's innate and inimitable gift for comic pantomime by choreographing for him *Danse Americaine* to music by Dent Mowrey. Nothing can give a clearer idea of this work than Weidman's own words as he wrote them in an article that appeared in *Dance Lovers Magazine* for June 1925:

This dance is purely pantomime. The costume is important to put your audience in the spirit of the dance from the moment you appear on stage. The suit is tightfitting, a vivid shade of tan. The shoes are the bulldog type, in yellow tan [i.e., blunt-toed, high-buttoned, thick-soled]. Light socks, striped shirt, bright tie, and derby.

The character is a small mill-town dude. He is the sport of the town and knows it. He is afraid of nothing on earth but the "skoits"! Remember to keep this spirit of bravado throughout the entire dance. There are no regular fixed steps: it is merely the interpretation of a story by gesture.

The soloist swaggers onstage and at once summons imaginary friends to admire his new clothes. He initiates a game of craps and wins everything. He joins a game of baseball in progress, first as pitcher, then as batter. After some mighty swings of the bat and two strikes, he tries for a home run but the umpire calls him out as he slides for third base. Dusting himself off in disgust, he turns away to bump into a beautiful girl. Shyly, he invites her to dance with him. To his surprise, she accepts. After a collision with another couple that nearly leads to a fight, the

Charles Weidman in *The Crapshooter.* The spirit of this dance, and its costume, were very similar to *Danse Americaine.* Photographed in performance at the Imperial Theatre, Tokyo, 1925. (Collection Jane Sherman)

dude does a show-off solo just for his girl—tap, clog, soft-shoe—any kind of dancing that comes into his head. The girl (and the real audience) applauds this exhibition so enthusiastically that he starts to leave without her. Then he remembers her and rushes back, full of apologies. Placing her arm in the crook of his, he gallantly leads her offstage, still gabbling excuses for his neglect.

The very first time Weidman did this solo (Apollo Theatre, Atlantic City, New Jersey, October 15, 1923) he had to give an encore. A writer for *Dance Lovers Magazine* observed, "One of the first real American dances we have ever seen. . . . There was something about it so different, so clever and so catchy that it seemed you must see it over and over again until you grasped every detail. Then you want to go home and try its popular sport steps yourself." (In 1936 Shawn incorporated other "sport steps" into the "Olympiad" section of his full-evening creation *O Libertad!*, when his Men Dancers performed "Decathalon," "Fencing," "Boxing," and "Basketball.")

Making its debut at the same time as *Danse Americaine* was a different view of Shawn's America: *Pasquinade* (or *A Creole Belle*), a solo he choreographed especially for Doris Humphrey. (This seems to be the first program on which Humphrey and Weidman appeared together, a portent of things to come.)

Humphrey was costumed completely in pink from her french-heeled satin slippers and ruffled, bustled long skirt with its satin bodice to the crown of the ostrich-feathered hat on her reddish hair. She enters on the first notes of a cakewalk composed by Louis Moreau Gottschalk. But this is a cakewalk as danced by a high-born New Orleans lady who minces on half-toes with a half-twist of her dainty feet, one hand held on her hip, the other outstretched before her as she proceeds in a very modified strut indeed. The nearest she comes to the more exuberant original is when she suddenly stops to flip up one foot high behind her as she tosses her head backward flirtatiously.

When the music picks up speed, she circles the stage with quick, floating, polka steps. With the repeat of the opening melody, she does a balletic turn at stage center, with high relevées on one foot as she flicks out the other on each beat. Maintaining this lighty, flittery mood, she exits with a backward kick of the leg, a broad smile, and a wink. This minor piece of sugary choreography created a certain spirit of a certain era in a certain place, and Humphrey most charmingly made her audiences believe in the character Shawn had formed for her.

He made himself into an outsize character of a cowboy in his 1924 *Around the Hall in Texas*, a duet that was always performed with *A*

Gringo Tango, both to music by Eastwood Lane. He wears flaring leather chaps with a holstered belt, high-heeled boots, exaggerated red bandanna around his neck, a dark blue cotton shirt, and a huge Stetson tilted to the back of his head. He enters with a bowlegged saunter to belly up to the bar of an imaginary dance hall of the old-time West. After tossing off a drink, he turns arrogantly to the hostess who approaches him. As played naughtily by Anne Douglas, she was the stereotype seen in Western movies of the day, in her high-buttoned pink kid boots, pink silk tights, brief full scarlet skirt, close-fitting waist, and high-piled blonde pompadour. Throwing aside his hat, the cowboy swings her into a bunny hug as they plunge into a fast spin around the dance floor. Every now and then the hostess breaks away from his hold to perform a miniature can-can of kicks and whirls, while the cowboy stamps in time to her antics, a-clapping and a-hollering and a-shooting his pistol at the wicked show of leg.

Into this raucous gaiety sways a handsome Mexican young woman costumed in a long black dress sashed by a brilliantly colored silk, fringed shawl, a scarlet scarf tied around her dark hair. Another stereotyped movie character, Ernestine Day had no difficulty attracting the cowboy's immediate attention. He drops his blonde hostess for this black-eyed siren, and they are soon clinging together in the kind of tango a "gringo" might conceive. No smooth tea dance, this. Cowboy and Chicana go swooping all over the stage, as he arches her into impossible backbends or swings her out into a twirl of black skirt, then grabs her close into a deep-kneed glide, pause, glide, abrupt turn. The rejected hostess interrupts this exotic display, and the cowboy gleefully grips her with a free hand. Stopping only long enough to clap his Stetson back on his head, he exits with an arm around each glamorous female, all three laughing.

For the 1930–1931 tour Shawn made with nine Denishawn Dancers but without St. Denis, he ventured into the area of American folk traditions with his *Four Dances Based on American Folk Music.* The following descriptions were provided by Barton Mumaw, a member of that Denishawn company and later the leading dancer in Shawn's Men Dancers for seven years. Mumaw not only saw Shawn perform these solos countless times but revived them for his own appearances at the Jacob's Pillow Dance Festival.

1. "Old Fiddler's Breakdown"
("Sheep 'n' Goat Walkin' to the Pasture")

Wearing only long tan work pants, his upper body also tan, the dancer shows off for two young ladies at a country barn dance. Throughout the solo he keeps his hands tucked into his trouser pockets as he struts through genre steps, stomps, and turns to pay attention first to one girl, then the other. About to leave without making up his mind which he prefers, he turns sharply, pulls his right hand out of his pocket and with it takes one of the girls offstage with him.

2. "Negro Spiritual" ("Nobody Knows de Trouble I've Seen")

A dance that mimes the helplessness of the slave and his ability to express pain through talking to God, this was the first, but not the last, of Shawn's explorations of Black culture. Many of the slow body movements are done on the floor, a technique that was new at the time the work was created.

3. "Methodist Revival Hymn" ("Give Me that Old-Time Religion")

Clapping rhythmically as he moves in a circle, the dancer expresses a joyous religious emotion in the revivalist tradition. Each conclusion of a chorus ends in a different manner, with a final movement-shout bursting into three spiral turns that end the solo with the dancer spread-eagled on the floor.

4. "Patriotic Song" ("Battle Hymn of the Republic")

The dancer is discovered bent over, his head looking up and diagonally forward, right foot advanced. As his body starts to straighten with the music, his foot beats in place, and both arms, extended parallel to each other, also rise. As if transfixed by a vision, he moves with long low steps to the diagonal front corner of the stage. There, with the musical phrase "Glory, glory Halleluiah," the man turns swiftly as he moves to center back, arms sweeping from full circles into a strong downward affirmative gesture. Facing the audience, he advances, as if he were leading great armies. His tread is heavy and measured until, near the footlights, he ends with a fall to both knees stretched widely apart, arms and torso straining outward and upward.

Music Visualizations

Ruth St. Denis has said that, inspired by Isadora Duncan's approach to music, she began to develop what she called music visualization, which she defined as ". . . the scientific translation into bodily action of the rhythmic, melodic and harmonious structure of a musical composition without intention to in any way 'interpret' or reveal any hidden meaning apprehended by the dancer." In an expanded form, notably Schubert's *Unfinished Symphony* for forty performers, presented at the fifth and last Lewisohn Stadium Denishawn concert in August, 1931, she attempted what she called a "synchoric orchestra." In this, groups of dancers strictly followed in movement that music being played by their assigned groups of instruments. Previously, St. Denis and Doris Humphrey had created something similar on a smaller scale in Beethoven's *Sonata Pathétique,* Schumann's *Soaring,* and MacDowell's *Sonata Tragica* (which was ultimately performed without any music whatsoever). Curiously, although music visualizations were presented in earlier concerts, the heading "Music Visualization" over the first part of a program did not appear until 1921 when Shawn made his own concert tour, assisted by Martha Graham, Betty May, Dorothea Bowen, and Charles Weidman, with Louis Horst as musical director. Here the several solos and trios listed had all been choreographed by Shawn.

St. Denis and Humphrey choreographed the first movement of Beethoven's piano sonata, opus 13 (the *Pathétique*) in 1919. Doris, as soloist, led a group of six girls, she following the right-hand melodies, they the left-hand accompaniment. Of course such a rigid format could

Martha Graham (far right) in the Music Visualization *Soaring.* This is a rare snapshot of Graham, taken during an outdoor rehearsal in preparation for the second Daniel Mayer United States Denishawn tour, 1923–1924. (Collection Jane Sherman)

not be maintained throughout and still sustain choreographic interest. As St. Denis wrote for a 1920 program note: "I have tried to get as much variety in the use of our instruments as possible, using one, two, or three figures, as well as the ensemble. Where a short solo is used it is meant to focus the attention a little more clearly on the individual passage or phrase, supplemented by the ensemble. Also where there is an emotional expression, even the dynamics of a large group can never equal the force of one individual's emotional capacity."

It was mainly Humphrey who captured these ideas in a choreographic form that "visualized" the music, as St. Denis once admitted she was the one more capable of doing. All seven dancers wore identical off-white chiffon chitons and bands around their heads, except Doris, whose hair was unbound. Upstage right (on audience left) the ensemble stands in a triangular grouping with Humphrey at the apex. On the first dramatic opening chord they take one step forward, simultaneously raising their arms shoulder-high and throwing back their heads. With the next notes they take corresponding step-step, step-pause, then bodies, heads and arms "wilt." This is repeated as the group turns to face back toward where it had started.

When the tempo quickens the dancers form two trios, as Doris stands alone at center stage. With arms around each others' waists they progress diagonally downstage in quick leap-steps, legs outstretched, bodies inclined backward. As certain themes are repeated so are the step formations, with Humphrey spinning a thread of brilliance through the ensemble as she responds to the piano's cadenzas. All motion halts midway in a frieze across the stage as the music abruptly stops. When it resumes its opening melodies, what seems to be a struggle among the ensemble, led by Doris, reaches a strong climax in a final frieze of poses that brings the work to a close. Many years later, after Humphrey, Graham, and Weidman had left Denishawn to develop their own techniques, St. Denis claimed, with some justice, that this rugged, original composition was the earliest suggestion of what became famous as American modern dance.

If I were to presume to choose which of her music visualizations came closest to Miss Ruth's heart, however, I would have to guess the *Brahms Waltz–Liszt Liebestraum* (always performed together). I say this because of the depth of feeling and integrity with which she always danced these works. Often there were tears in her own eyes at the end, as well as in the eyes of many in her audience. Simply done to simple, familiar music, the soloist wears a long, soft, silken pale blue Grecian gown with a large scarf of the same material across her back extending over her arms from shoulders to fingertips. Her silvery hair is dressed in the slightly bouffant style she wore offstage. For the nostalgic but lilting Brahms waltz in A flat major, she moves in a pinkish spotlight against a blue background, seeming to float rather than step. She pauses only to "pat" the air with both hands, first on one side then the other, with the accented notes of that melodic phrase.

Before applause can break out at the end of the waltz, the first notes of the Liszt are heard while the lighting deepens to a violet blue. Miss Ruth's face wears a mask of sorrow as, with outstretched arms and tender fingers, she seeks her lost love. Toward the finish of the dance she takes a few hesitant steps to the right, holding out her right hand in a gesture of pleading that is infinitely touching. She repeats this to the left. Then, as if accepting unendurable pain, she joins both hands and buries her head in the scarf that covers her arms as they reach out before her toward the wings when she leaves the stage. (It was said that after the earliest performances of this work, Shawn was always waiting for her there to carry her to her dressing-room.)

Shawn's first ensemble music visualization was choreographed, prophetically, for six men: himself, Weidman, and four others. *Polonaise,* to music by Edward MacDowell, remained in his repertory through the Men Dancers' 1938 series of concerts at the Majestic Theatre in New York. His next music visualization was a stunning solo, *The Death of Adonis,* to Godard's composition *Adagio Pathétique.* Based on the antique statues he had admired during his first trip to Europe, he built a so-called sculpture plastique that told the story of how Adonis was killed by a boar while out hunting. Shawn planned to wear no more than a figleaf, a white, close-fitting curled wig, and a coat of white body paint.

This was extremely daring for the day. Audiences had seen living statue acts in vaudeville, where men and women, dressed (or undressed) as statues, held fixed poses for a brief instant before the lights blacked out. Until Shawn attempted it, however, no one in this country had yet seen nudity combined with movement. It was too shocking for the cook at Mariarden, the art colony where Shawn was to premiere this work. When she saw the dress rehearsal, she frantically phoned her employers to inform them that Mr. Shawn was doing an obscene dance. After the owners of Mariarden saw *Adonis* in rehearsal for themselves, they agreed it was sheer artistry with no hint of obscenity. But they also feared their New England summer theatre subscribers might find it a bit too unusual, so they permitted Shawn, instead, to perform it just for a selected private audience. Only after it had then received the first of the ovations it was invariably to receive during its long lifetime, did *Adonis* earn a place on the regular program.

Shawn confined the movements of his solo to a large white circular platform placed deep upstage. At one edge, on a "marble" tree stump the nearly nude, motionless figure is discovered seated at curtain rise. In a dim blue lighting that lends dignity and verisimilitude to the classic poses, the dancer moves with an intense control that creates the illusion of a statue come to life. The work and its effect on audiences cannot better be summed up than by quoting a critic in the *Calcutta Statesman* for April 6, 1926: "First among these brilliant solos, and probably first in the whole company's repertoire, is Ted Shawn's *Adagio Pathétique.* . . . This astonishing piece of rhythmic motion, wherein the use of the lower limbs is reduced to a minimum and the greater part of the effect produced by the swaying of the trunk, is artistic to the last degree. In three or four minutes, the dancer succeeds in conveying the whole of the tense tragedy around which the music is written." *Adonis* was last performed in 1930.

Many Denishawn works employed the trio form, and of these one of the loveliest was a 1919 music visualization St. Denis choreographed for Doris Humphrey, Claire Niles, and Betty May to Debussy's *Second Arabesque.* When I danced this with Ernestine Day and Anne Douglas for the first Lewisohn Stadium concert in 1925 and throughout the Orient tour, we wore ankle-length, faintly tawny-colored Grecian chiffon tunics banded with elastic at the waist. Each head was adorned by a dark red wig of real hair piled into a curled topknot and held in place by three narrow satin ribbons.

The mood of the dance is as light-hearted as the music. The dancers match their swift, bouncy steps on half-toe to the swift, bouncy triplets of Debussy's opening melody as they move downstage in a rosy lighting. They maintain a unity of three with arms arched or intertwined, as seen in so many paintings of figures on Greek vases. When the music slows, two of the trio separate from the central dancer, one to a side. With a slow, sweeping turn, bodies bend forward as arms parallel the pointed, circling foot. Obeying Miss Ruth's dictum that "A joyous lyric dance like *Second Arabesque* should radiate physical joy. . . ." the dancers hop in what she called a fish step: in sequence with the repeated musical theme, first one dancer flicks up her leg at knee height in back while at the same instant flicking her hands outward from chest level, then the next, then the third, until all meet to join hands in a circle. Skipping lightly upstage into a line facing in profile to the right, they step precisely on each final staccato note from the piano: an arabesque with the left leg, a hold on right half-toe, a pose with the left foot crossing the right, a lifting of both hands to fold at the chest, a demure dropping of heads just as the rosy lights fade.

Anne Douglas danced a charming music visualization solo that had only a brief professional life, but once seen, was not easily forgotten. To the opening bars of Chopin's *Minute Waltz*, she runs onstage in a lavender, ankle-length Grecian tunic designed with a delicately flared circular skirt. Her hair is bound close to her head with satin lavender bands. Both hands are held cupped high beneath her chin. On the first note of the first melody, she opens her hands to release a pair of long lavender satin ribbons three to four inches wide. One end of a ribbon is fastened to each shoulder, with the opposite end held in each hand. The dancer twirls into a swift spin, arms and ribbons held out at shoulder height. She arabesques to the left, then to the right, flipping the ribbons over her shoulders at the same moment.

Like a child playing on a garden lawn, she runs diagonally downstage, holding the ribbons so they float high behind her. With the quiet musical middle theme, she moves diagonally backward to center stage using a combination that consists of a slow step, a lift of the leg to the front, one arm parallel and the other behind, and repeat. After a long spin in place, spiraling the ribbons from knees to overhead, she repeats the opening formations. At the end, she runs directly toward the audience from upstage, ribbons arching like wings behind her. With a flip of the ribbons over each arm, she holds a brief pose. Then she runs gaily offstage, the ribbons trailing after her like silken comets.

Valse à La Loie was a favorite with audiences from the first time Geordie Graham and Anne Douglas performed it in 1924 to the last time they did it in 1927. The duo was created by St. Denis as a tribute to her fellow-American dancer Loie Fuller, whose use of lights and fabrics she had greatly admired when she saw Fuller dance in France in the early 1900s. Miss Ruth clad her two Denishawn Dancers only in flesh-colored leotards, worn with straw-colored wigs bobbed in a Dutch cut. Around the shoulders of each she suspended a floor-length, very full circular white silk cape. This was open in the front and held firmly in each hand. Except in some particularly vigorous movements, the material covered the arms and most of the body. Unlike Fuller, who had often depended on thin wands with which to manipulate her fabric, St. Denis shaped her capes into varied forms by using only the hands and arms of her dancers.

This dance, as intended, was strictly impersonal. Limbs and bodies merged with the yards of silk as if they were integral parts of each other. In the changing colors of the lights and the figurations of the material, even faces were often invisible. The duo that thus emerged took the form of a strong, happy Rorschach test in vivid tints and constant motion. The lighting, as well as the steps, followed the structure and the varying moods of the Chopin waltz, opus 14 (posth).

At opening, the stage is faintly lit with a blueish purple background. Against this, reddish following spots pick up each dancer as one enters from upper stage right and one from upper stage left in a series of low turns and floating fabric that meet at stage center with the upthrust of two waves clashing. Subtly changing warm colors engulf the two figures as they skip diagonally and turn, arms high, bend toward each other then away, or face the audience side by side to raise and lower their arms like butterfly wings.

With the gentle, slower second theme, the two move together diagonally downstage in a deliberate step-extend, brief run, and fling the silk backward with their outside arms; a step-extend, brief run, and fling the silk forward. Here the lights alter to pastel flower hues that focus on the petal shapes. During a series of slow pas de basques, the fabric next drifts like reeds seen under water in a bluegreen lighting. After another strong flight of butterfly wings, the lighting changes to flame. The dancers spiral swiftly in place before sweeping to opposite sides of the stage. There they approach the climax of extremely fast turns, arms winging up and down. With a last leap and a final run they meet at center in a high jump, then fall flat on the stage away from each other in a pool of crimson light that immediately blacks out.

In 1926 Shawn choreographed a music visualization entitled *Choeur Dansé* to music of the same name by N. Stcherbatcheff (opus 8, number 10). This plotless, slightly humorous work was created for Ernestine Day, Anne Douglas, and Geordie Graham (whose part I later danced). Quite brief, it was almost over before the audience realized it, but they loved it from its first performance at the Victoria Theatre in Singapore on July 15, 1926, to its last in Carnegie Hall on April 6, 1927.

The music with its unusual 9/8, 7/8, 9/8 time changes, inspired the antiphonal form of the trio Shawn designed. Center girl (A) first danced the "statement," then her companions B and C danced the "response." Because of the off-white, short, silk costume tunics worn, the impression might have been Grecian, but the formations, the spirit, always seemed more like three fawns gamboling, each alert to the others and to possible danger. (See Appendix for complete choreographic notes.)

Choeur Dansé was one of the few Denishawn group dances that Shawn reworked for his Men Dancers. Under the title *Choric Dance from an Antique Greek Comedy,* it was first programmed in its all-male version for the 1934–1935 United States tour, with Barton Mumaw as dancer A and Wilbur McCormack and Dennis Landers as B and C. The choreography remained essentially the same as the original, but the style was more vigorous, with stronger leaps, higher hops on half-toes, and more rigorously accented hands, elbows, and knees bent at right angles to the body in the two-dimensional poses and figurations.

The costumes were different, of course. Each man wore high-waisted trunks of a sturdy gold-colored material to which were appliquéd overlapping plates of the same material to simulate gold-leaf armor. These harmonized with their golden tan body paint under amber lighting to create a vivid image of three Grecian statues brought to life.

This dance was also programmed for the London engagement of the Men Dancers in the spring of 1935, when the distinguished critic and balletomane Arnold Haskell wrote, "Better ensemble dancing I have seldom seen, and not merely on account of persistent rehearsal, but because each person has an unusually developed musical sense." Anton Dolin, the famous danseur of the Sadler's Wells Ballet, later known as the Royal Ballet, attended all eleven London performances. He told Shawn that England's male dancers had now seen how men should move, and could never again get away with the kind of dancing with which they had previously been content.

The *Choric Dance from an Antique Greek Comedy* was last performed on the Men Dancers' 1935–1936 United States tour. American critics who had earlier been skeptics then wrote of Shawn's music visualizations opinions such as, "The dancers were remembered as being like scattered notes from a hidden keyboard, so perfect was their interpretation of the music;" and, ". . . striking geometric arrangements, the exquisitely balanced groupings;" and, "Music, movement, technique and symbolism are thoroughly synthesized into a harmonious medium of thought, feeling and decoration."

Miscellanea

In the early days of Denishawn, audiences were conditioned by vaudeville, concerts, and annual pupil recitals to dance programs made up of solos, duets, trios, or small ensembles. Not until the 1916 tour of Diaghilev's Ballets Russes did the privileged audiences of large American cities witness dance productions of greater length and depth. Not until the 1919–1921 two-a-day vaudeville tours made by Shawn's three-act *Julnar of the Sea* and his two-act *Xochitl* were the inhabitants of our smaller towns and cities able to see full-length ballets. Even when Denishawn concert programs came to present long ballets, they continued to include the ever-popular shorter works. Many of these do not fit neatly into pigeonholes labeled "Oriental," "American," or "Music Visualization;" the following are thumbnail descriptions of a few of these Denishawn divertissements.

In 1917 the minister of the First Interdenominational Church of San Francisco invited Ted Shawn to perform his *Church Service in Dance.* Here, after his years of giving ballroom dance exhibitions, Shawn, the preacher-turned-actor-dancer, came into his true element. Following the minister's half-hour history of the relationship of dance to religion, the young, handsome dancer appears before the simple altar. His thick, dark hair cut at earlobe length is brushed back severely from his forehead. He is dressed in white from head to slippers, with a high-necked, long-sleeved top and long trousers. Hanging from his shoulders he wears a full, dark, sleeveless cape that resembles a priest's chasuble.

Accompanied by the string section of the San Francisco Symphony Orchestra, he dances with great dignity and reverence, a Prayer to an excerpt from *Kammenoi Ostrow.* There follow a Doxology and Gloria, and The Twenty-third Psalm. A symbolic sermon, "Ye shall know the Truth and the Truth shall make you free," is danced to the Rachmaninoff C-sharp minor Prelude. After a Hymn, "Beulah Land," the program ends with a Benediction, "God be with you till we meet again." The large audience and the newspaper reviewers treated the service with all seriousness. This was particularly gratifying to Shawn because it marked his last public appearance before he joined the army ambulance corps of World War I.

In 1918, with her "Best Beloved Teddy" in the Army and the war still on, Ruth St. Denis, with Doris Humphrey, three other dancers, and Louis Horst, was booked on a coast-to-coast-and-return tour of the Pantages vaudeville circuit (three performances a day, with four on Saturdays and Sundays). Their mini-concert program included a Siamese ballet to music by Horst and a *Greek Scene* consisting of the trio *Second Arabesque,* a solo for Humphrey entitled *Dance of the Sunrise,* and the St. Denis solo *Greek Veil Plastique.*

Here the tall, beautiful dancer is costumed in a medium length off-white chiton that is held below the bosom with three bands of elastic spaced a few inches apart. She wears a blonde wig parted in the center into waves close to her head, its ends curled à la Greque at the back of the neck. To music by Gluck, she moves in what Denishawn had developed as a sculpture plastique, wherein motion progresses simply and without pause from one pose to the next. With every movement she skillfully manipulates a very large circular white silk veil that is bordered in black with a Greek key design.

Sometimes she poses holding one edge of the veil high above her head, the rest of the material rising from its small pool at her feet in a long fold that follows the lines of her arched body. Sometimes she arranges the circle of fabric so that it falls before her in sculptured folds, covering her body and arms entirely as she raises her hands out to each side, palms up. She bends her head slightly to the left and forward, as if seeing herself reflected in still water. (It was this pose, with Miss Ruth standing on the rim of a real pond, that the noted photographer Arnold Genthe preserved for posterity.)

The mood is dignified and gracious as St. Denis demonstrates the masterful handling of drapery that was the hallmark of much of her choreography. Both in the sculptural and the Grecian senses, she seems to have been influenced here (as in so many of her works) by the Delsartist Genevieve Stebbins. In 1892, when Ruthie Dennis was only thirteen, she had been taken to a matinee given by Mrs. Stebbins, where she saw her move as a figure of Greek sculpture. St. Denis was later to call this experience "the real birth of my art life," the first spiritual and artistic dancer she had ever seen.

In 1921 Shawn went out on a concert tour with Martha Graham, Charles Weidman, Betty May, Dorothea Bowen, and Louis Horst. The program opened with his *Church Service in Dance*, which he performed this time with the three female dancers. It continued with twenty-four solos, trios, duets, and ensembles, and concluded with the ballet *Xochitl*. Listed under "Music Visualizations" was a veritable hodgepodge of brief numbers, many of which could not truly be so categorized. One of these was an odd little trio called *Juba*.

This work can best be described in Shawn's own words from his book *One Thousand and One Night Stands:* "I created a light comedy number with Martha as an old mammy, Betty May and Dorothea as pickaninnies, using for accompaniment Nathaniel Dett's '*Juba Dance*.' It was the first dance use made of Dett's lively tune now so hackneyed."

The author has seen a snapshot taken of the dancers in *Juba*. It shows a grinning Graham, her head wrapped in a bandanna, her arms around two timid, crouching figures, and all three costumed in cotton dresses that seem on the verge of rags. Suzanne Shelton has told me that she believes this dance was performed in blackface. I find this difficult to accept if only because it would require too much time for the makeup to be removed and replaced for the next dances in which the three were to perform. In any case, dance historians might well ignore this opus except as a curiosity in which the early Graham briefly appeared.

Among their miscellanea may rightfully be placed Denishawn's Spanish dances. There were, in addition to the ballet *Cuadro Flamenco*, several interesting works in this genre that had been principally inspired by Shawn's studies with outstanding teachers in Seville and Barcelona. Although Spanish technique was not her strong point, St. Denis starred in *Cuadro Flamenco,* danced the duet *Malagueña* with Shawn (which he also performed with Graham), and did at least one lovely Spanish solo. This last was her *Shawl Plastique*, also known as *Danza Español*, which Shawn created for her in 1922 to music by Granados.

Now the chameleon-like St. Denis assumes a saucy, arrogant air when she enters in her long, white costume with its form-fitting bodice and ruffled skirt and sleeves, a magnificent Spanish shawl draped around her shoulders. Her black wig flaunts a tall comb. On her feet are black, low-heeled, strapped shoes. As the dance progresses, it becomes obvious that there is little attempt beyond this costuming to re-create an actual Spanish dance. What St. Denis does create is the atmosphere of bygone Spain through courtly yet casual and earthy movements as she dances with the shawl as if with a human partner. Her beautiful arms and supple back are arched at the proper moments. One's attention is mesmerized by her facial expressions and by the shapes into which she imperceptibly but strongly molds the embroidered shawl to the rhythms and melodies of the Granados music. An enchanting moment.

By contrast, Shawn's *Flamenco Dances* approach the authentic as nearly as was possible for a tall, big-boned, heavy man. In his skin-tight black silk Andalusian trousers, brief jacket, white shirt, and black broad-brimmed hat, his entrance causes a startled gasp of delight. To music from Spanish manuscripts that had been transcribed by Horst, this handsome caballero starts his dance with a slow, steady clapping of his hands as he regards his audience with cold arrogance. The tempo picks up, the rhythms change, the clapping becomes stamping, the arrogance turns inward. The solo reaches a frenzy of intricate heel

beats, clapping, finger-snapping, tongue-clicking, swift turns with deep
backbends, outrageous flirting with an imaginary partner, and all the
wildness of a Triana gypsy expressing his spirit through physical motion. This ends abruptly with the dancer lunging deeply to one bent
knee, the other leg straight out behind him on the floor, as he holds his
hat high over his head and faces the theatre with a fierce stare. Invariably, the audience response was so enthusiastic that Shawn had to
do one or more encores, shedding hat, then jacket, then tie in the
process.

These series of dances were a big hit in the *Follies,* but perhaps never
so big as when Shawn performed them in 1921 in Martha Graham's
hometown of Santa Barbara, where Martha danced the *Malagueña*
with him. At the instant of Shawn's final lunge in *Flamenco Dances,* his
trousers split up the back seam with a loud explosion. The embarrassed
dancer had to back off the stage, holding his hat behind him. Next day, a
local newspaper reviewer reported that "The prayer of a lifetime was
answered when incredibly tight Spanish trousers burst wide open during last night's performance."

On one of the four programs St. Denis and Shawn took to the Orient,
under the heading of "Divertissements" were eight numbers, of which
two were ensemble dances: *Garland Plastique* and *Bubble Dance.* In
1925, St. Denis choreographed *Garland Plastique* for five dancers to
music by Schubert, as an introduction to her own solos of waltzes by the
same composer.

All the dancers wear the long Denishawn chiton, with bands of
chiffon around their hair. They enter upstage left in a line, holding
hands and also holding a single long garland of flowers that falls in
gentle loops between them. This garland never leaves their hands as the
dancers walk rhythmically to the slow music, forming diagonals, circles, and groupings. Now they stop to pose with the garland held
overhead. Then they continue their plastique of gentle walk and formations until they end in a line down front across the stage. The center
figure holds the middle of the garland above her head. The dancers
directly on either side of her fondé with the garland held in both hands
at shoulder height. The outer pair of dancers lie half upright on the floor
so that the frieze forms a pyramid. As with many Denishawn works, a
prop (in this instance the garland) becomes the center around which the
entire dance is built.

The props in *Bubble Dance* were, as might be expected, balloons. To
music by Wenk, Shawn had dreamed up this bit of dance play in 1925

especially for the Orient tour. Six female dancers in flesh-colored leotards and Dutch-bobbed blonde wigs cavort under ever-changing colored lights with a large assortment of different-colored balloons some two feet in diameter. The dance is so determined by the erratic behavior of these air bubbles that the dancers must perforce improvise around the choreography. A puff of wind from the wings blows a balloon out of reach of upheld hands. Another's unexpected descent in a dancer's path causes her to veer and stumble. In pursuit of the same elusive balloon, two dancers narrowly avoid collision.

Through all this disorganized activity, the performers try to maintain assured, smiling faces to keep the illusion that everything is going as intended, that they merely represent children enjoying a game. But when the balloons soon touch the hot footlights and burst, or when they come near the even hotter arc lights in the wings to explode with a bang, it is hard for audience and dancers alike not to break into unpremeditated laughter. Fortunately for the reputation of Denishawn, as balloon after balloon burst, stage manager Brother St. Denis ran out of the irreplaceable supply he had brought from the States. To everyone's considerable relief, the number had to be removed from the program and was never, to my knowledge, performed again.

In trying to envision even these few dances selected from the three hundred and fifty-odd in the Denishawn repertory, the reader should be made aware of an admonition that Doris Humphrey repeatedly gave students and company members alike: "Always be strong. Never be 'pretty.'" If this is kept in mind, one of the most prevalent and persistent misconceptions about Denishawn may be corrected. For even in the daintiest characterization or the most light-hearted divertissement, St. Denis, Shawn, and their dancers performed with strength, dignity, and conviction. It is doubtful if any dance company then or since has been called on to perform so many different techniques or to convey so many different musical and dramatic moods and ethnic qualities.

Chapter Five

Denishawn in Vaudeville and Beyond

WITH SERIOUS DANCE BEING presented today in lofts, concert halls, films, television, universities, churches, temples, schools, and museums, it is difficult to realize that when Ruthie Dennis started her career at age fifteen, such opportunities to find audiences were few and far between. Ballet at the Metropolitan Opera represented the dance Mecca in this country, but little Ruth did not aim that high. She made her New York debut in a structure called Worth's Family Theatre and Museum. Although it was considered respectable, this establishment hardly merited its pretentious title. There, amid monstrous pickled animal freaks displayed in glass containers and between lectures on historical relics, Dennis did a skirt dance six times a day on a program of variety acts.

It was from such ambiences as Worth's Museum, minstrel shows, burlesque shows, and roof gardens that vaudeville developed. (The name is a distortion of the French *Vau-de-Vire,* meaning valley of the Vire, a river in Normandy where the populace was noted for its light songs.) This new form of entertainment combined the artistry *(sic)* of its predecessors, featuring a show consisting of as many as ten or twelve different acts, each show presented two, three, or even four times a day. At first, vaudeville toured what primitive theatres then existed in the country, bringing big-city theatricalism to unsophisticated audiences. As it grew more and more profitable, however, managerial chains built their own theatres in the larger cities, for example, Proctor's, Pantage's, and B. F. Keith's. The acts they booked into their new palaces improved, principally because the Broadway revue, which was developing about the same time, provided both fields of entertainment with interchangeable star performances by dancers, singers, and comics, by acrobats,

animal acts, and magicians. In this same period, the American musical
comedy, as distinct from the European operetta, was also coming into
its own and providing still more jobs for dancers.

Ruthie gained her theatrical experience in all these areas long before
she found her own true way of dancing, even as Shawn found his
through ballroom-dance exhibitions. Indeed, St. Denis hit on her idea
for *Radha* while she was working to create a new vaudeville dance. That
was when she began her serious exploration of Hindu mythology and
history, as she read books and visited bona fide museums to study East
Indian paintings and sculpture.

With the financial help of family and friends that enabled her to buy
costumes, set, and lighting, the first great vision of St. Denis was finally
realized. *Radha* was performed and applauded in the salon of a society
lady whose guests invariably included writers, painters, and musicians.
After several equally successful appearances at other private soirees,
Ruth St. Denis made her true professional debut as a serious soloist in
1906, when she was booked to perform *Radha* on a vaudeville program
that opened at the New York Theatre. She then took *Radha* to Washington, D.C., to Boston's famous Fenway Court, home of Mrs. Jack
Gardner, and, as a climax, to the Duchess of Manchester's house in
London. From there, for three years St. Denis toured England, France,
Germany (including a royal command performance at Weimar), Aus-
tria, Belgium, Hungary, and Monte Carlo. Everywhere she was received as a great artist.

On her return to this country in 1909 St. Denis continued for years to
alternate vaudeville dates with appearances in the homes of high society
or before women's clubs, adding Japanese and Egyptian works to her
famed East Indian repertory. After she married Ted Shawn in 1914 and
they formed the first Denishawn school, their subsequent concerts
together were so popular that the two with their Denishawn Dancers
were offered many vaudeville engagements, the most lucrative of which
they accepted because they needed income to support the school, the
company, and new productions.

Given the descriptions of some of the Denishawn dances for which St.
Denis and Shawn were famous, the idea that these works could have
been presented in vaudeville may seem incredible. Yet the fact remains
that for all Denishawners of that era vaudeville provided both audiences
and life-sustaining funds at various periods of their lives. For their
coast-to-coast tours on the two-a-day Orpheum, Keith, or Pantages
circuits, these artists adamantly refused to compromise their standards

to win the approval of people who had come principally to see tap dancers, blues singers, and other run-of-the-mill acts. Even if those audiences failed to appreciate the unfamiliar Denishawn pearl on the program, they had to swallow it to eat the oyster.

In this way, thousands of Americans across the country who had never before seen serious dancing became dance-educated in spite of themselves. In 1916, St. Denis, Shawn, and company were even booked into New York's prestigious Palace Theatre—that ultimate goal of every star such as George Burns and Gracie Allen, the Marx Brothers, and Jack Benny. To the amazement of all concerned, so many people had to be turned away at the box-office that the management kept Denishawn on for a second week. Except for Sarah Bernhardt, this was the only act to that time that had ever been held over at the Palace.

In vaudeville, the Denishawn mini-concert was presented midway in a long program of conventional acts. One concert offered St. Denis in *The Spirit of the Sea* (as a solo), Ada Forman in *Danse Javanese,* Shawn in *The Thunderbird,* and the entire company in a Moorish ballet entitled *The Peacock.* Another concert featured a St. Denis Japanese flower arrangement and her *Cobras,* an ensemble called *Nature Rhythms,* and a *Ballet of Ancient Egypt.* Louis Horst was, as usual, at the piano.

This was indeed gourmet fare for plebian tastes, yet audiences devoured it greedily for fifty-six weeks of one-night stands in 1916–1917. For a 1918 vaudeville tour with Doris Humphrey and a group of young women, St. Denis ventured to present Grecian solos and trios to music by Debussy and Gluck, a *Siamese Ballet,* and a stirring war-time *Spirit of Democracy,* which she danced to Chopin's *Revolutionary Étude.* The program of one such tour lists the Denishawn act followed by "Fannie Brice, Comedienne."

For artists with dreams of what dance could be, vaudeville was uninspiring, almost degrading, labor. Shawn described the management representatives from agents and bookers to local theatre managers as, ". . . the most sadistic, ghoulish, and horrible people encountered in a long professional life," adding, "those [in the audience] who spent hard-earned quarters to watch a seal twirl a trumpet were not *always* receptive to the dance of Denishawn. Against odds we made friends for the art of the dance, and sparked applause by our sweat and sincerity. We gave our best at every performance." This best arose from the devout belief of St. Denis and Shawn in dance as a great and important art. When she was quite old, Miss Ruth once told Walter Terry that she wished all young dancers would be compelled to have the experience of touring in vaudeville, not only for the discipline but to learn that, "you have to get your audience within the first thirty seconds of your appearance on stage. It was easier in concert because there you had *sixty* seconds!"

During layoffs, Miss Ruth and Papa taught at their Los Angeles school and made forays into the concert field, alone or together, but until the first Daniel Mayer United States tour of 1922–1923, vaudeville provided their basic bread and butter. Alexander Pantages commissioned an act for his circuit, and Shawn created *Julnar of the Sea.* This was an Arabian Nights spectacle in three scenes, with a cast of seventeen gorgeously costumed dancers and a narrator to make the story clear to audiences who had never heard of Scheherazade. With Horst as pianist-conductor, *Julnar* took to the road in November 1919 and played continuously until March 1921. Later that year Shawn sent out another vaudeville company in his Aztec ballet *Xochitl.* This featured a young Martha Graham and an even younger Charles Weidman, with eight girl dancers. Pauline Lawrence, the future partner of Humphrey and Weidman and wife of José Limón, was at the piano. Critics called this work "the first native American ballet," and audiences loved watching the pure but fiery Graham fight off the evil advances of Weidman's Emperor Tepancáltzin.

During this era, individual Denishawn Dancers and students also began to impress audiences in vaudeville and Broadway revues. Vanda Hoff starred in the vaudeville production of *The Dancing Girl of Delhi* before she met and married bandleader Paul Whiteman. In the 1923 *Greenwich Village Follies,* the engagement that marked her break with Denishawn, Martha Graham performed Shawn's swift, seductive *Serenata Morisca.* Florence O'Denishawn appeared in the 1921 *Ziegfeld Follies* and in the 1923 *Music Box Revue,* doing a famous dance in which her slender body, clad only in nude fleshings and a few leaves, represented a bending, swaying, quivering eucalyptus tree.

She had been plain Florence Andrews as a Denishawn company member during the concert and vaudeville tours of 1915–1917. Then, as Shawn reports in *One Thousand and One Night Stands,* "I created a dozen dances for her, financed costuming and a publicity campaign for a night-club act which I also booked. Her name was uninteresting and since Denishawn by then was nationally famous, I suggested that she call herself Florence of Denishawn. She did until a program printing error made Florence O'Denishawn of her. At the height of her success in night clubs, Florence was spotted by the famous comedian, Raymond Hitchcock, who started her toward Broadway by signing her for *Hitchy-Koo.*"

As may no longer be remembered, there was another popular field for dancers in those days. Many motion picture theatres were enormous, ornate palaces complete with stage, lighting equipment, flies for scenery, orchestra pits, and velvet or gold brocade curtains to rival those of the finest opera houses. In New York City, some of these theatres even had their own permanent dancing chorus, such as the Roxyettes at the Roxy, the Chester Hale Girls at the Capitol, and later the Rockettes at Radio City Music Hall. Before the feature film was shown, at least once an afternoon and twice at night there was presented a small show called a prologue. Lasting from one-half to three-quarters of an hour, this usually consisted of a musical overture, a singer, a solo dancer, and a group dancing a finale.

Many then well-known Denishawn dancers found work in this area. Lillian Powell danced *Tunisienne* at New York's Criterion, and tiny, big-eyed Marjorie Peterson danced a *Valse Ballet* at the Rivoli. It was during those years that the Denishawn school advertised that a professional dancer could have a solo choreographed exclusively for her for the high price of $200, including costume and music. It is therefore certain that many less talented dancers invaded the vaudeville, revue, and prologue fields with these creations. In addition to the continuing appearances of St. Denis and Shawn, it was because of such activity that Denishawn became mainly responsible for the introduction of serious dance into popular theatre. For as they improved the technique of their pupils and the material of their choreography, they improved the taste of audiences. The record seems to bear this out. By 1926 the *Earl Carroll Vanities* featured ballets by Anton Dolin. The *Ziegfeld Follies* topped this with ballets by the great Fokine in 1927, and its 1936 edition boasted choreography by none other than Balanchine.

Denishawn influence was felt in another way: they were the first American company to raise the male dancer to the equal of the female in duets and ensembles. Long before he formed his Men Dancers in 1933, Shawn had insisted, "We will not reach the pinnacle of greatness that dance is capable of until we have as many men in dance companies and as soloists as we have women." Can anyone today imagine a Broadway, Hollywood, or television musical without its contingent of wonderful male dancers? (In the 1960s, after Gene Kelly had done a television special called *Dancing Is a Man's Game,* Shawn met and congratulated him, saying, "You have helped the cause I have given my life to." Kelly replied with his engaging grin, "I know. When I saw you and your Men Dancers perform at my high school in Pittsburgh, that started me being a dancer.")

There is also a matter of priority that is interesting to explore. Denishawn's ethnic and Americana dances won wide approval long before this material could be discerned in the Broadway theatre. For instance, Shawn's Hopi Indian ballet considerably predated Tamiris's exciting Indian dances in *Annie Get Your Gun* (in which Barton Mumaw, incidentally, played the lead dancer in the Mary Martin company). The 1922 Denishawn *Siamese Ballet* toured the United States years before the charming dances of *The King and I* were seen on stage or film. St. Denis's Japanese *O-Mika* of 1915 and Shawn's 1926 Kabuki dance-drama *Momiji-Gari* preceded the musical *Pacific Overtures* by many seasons. *Boston Fancy: 1854* and the cowboy romp *Around the Hall in Texas* were applauded all over the country twenty years prior to Agnes de Mille's epoch-making choreography for *Oklahoma!*.

Denishawn's most direct connection to the world of Broadway was probably made when St. Denis, Shawn, and their Dancers were starred in a road company of the *Ziegfeld Follies* in 1927–1928. They accepted the engagement only because their large salary as the featured attraction would enable them to finance the building of their new school near Van Cortlandt Park in New York.

This was the closest I ever came to dancing in vaudeville, and neither I nor the other six girls and two boys with Denishawn realized what we were getting into. Ours was not a national touring company of the *Follies;* it was what was known as a "tab" show, a hodgepodge put together by an arrangement under which an out-of-town producer bought the *Ziegfeld Follies* title, with some of the sketches and elaborate sets and costumes from previous editions, but without the original famous stars. Those in our *Follies,* we quickly learned, were unknown singers and comics who had graduated from vaudeville or burlesque. The boys and girls of the chorus were recruited from small-town dance schools or from among those unfortunate "gypsies" who had been rejected in the casting of Broadway musicals. The showgirls had been personally selected by our producer, George Wintz, from local beauty-contest winners. When some of these left the show during the tour for one reason or another, Mr. Wintz would replace them with pretty young saleswomen or waitresses whom he lured from their mundane jobs in

Ernestine Day and Jane Sherman playing at being *Ziegfeld Follies* dancers during rehearsals in Dayton, Ohio, for the Denishawn *Follies* tour of 1927–1928. (Collection Jane Sherman)

small towns or provincial cities by the glamorous promise of the Ziegfeld name.

With our prim, idealistic backgrounds, we Denishawners felt like a flock of black crows among a covey of brilliant jungle parrots when first we met the full *Follies* company one hot day in a rehearsal hall in Dayton, Ohio. Even though we were the stars of this adventure, we were to share dressing-rooms, train coaches, hotels, and stages with these exotic creatures for forty weeks of an intimacy that considerably broadened our education. We heard language we had never imagined in all our sheltered lives. We witnessed behavior we had never dreamed possible. Here in the middle of Prohibition days, we saw more drinking than we could believe. Even more alarming, our dances were surrounded by a distressing environment.

We had expected that our capsule concert of some ten numbers might logically be presented as a featured act, but instead our dances were programmed throughout the show. Right after a burlesque sketch called "Mental Telepathy" came our first number, the bacchanale *Allegresse* to music by Sinding. Following a slapstick comedy duo, Miss Ruth did her solo *The Dance of the Red and Gold Sari.* As part of the first-act finale, a huge production number set in a Parisian cafe, Shawn performed his *Flamenco Dances.* After something called "The Blue Blue's Stomp Dance" came our *Soaring,* that delicate creation for five girls who wore silk flesh-colored leotards and danced with a large square veil under varicolored lights to music by Robert Schumann. This was immediately followed by St. Denis's poignant *Waltz-Liebestraum.* And when a chorus line had tapped through the "Kickiekick," the lights went down for Shawn's *Cosmic Dance of Siva*! After this had invariably stopped the show, and the star comedienne had finished her speciality act, Miss Ruth did her famous *Nautch.* Then we all joined her in an East Indian mini-ballet.

For ten months this was our routine, night after night, and twice a day with matinees. There was no time or strength to attend class or rehearse. No new dances were created. We could afford to buy few new books because we were all either saving as much money as possible or sending a goodly share home to help support our families. No new friends were to be made among the members of the *Follies* company since our interests were as far apart as the north and south poles.

On the *Follies* private train, the principals had compartments while the musicians, stagehands, show girls, chorines, and Denishawners piled into two day coaches. Most of our departures took place before dawn so we could reach the next town in time to hang that night's show. We therefore quickly learned how to lower the back of a double seat to make a flat bed. Then we pulled out the baby pillow each of us carried and snuggled down under our coats to sleep until the stage manager came through the car calling "Fifteen minutes! Fifteen minutes!" to arrival. In the so-called theatres, the school auditoriums, the rodeo arenas, and the convention centers where we played, the stars occupied whatever dressing-rooms existed. The rest of us made do in locker rooms, basements, hallways, and, once or twice, even in walled platforms that had been built out into the street behind the stage especially to accommodate us. When the chorus girls discovered that local men-about-town were spying on them through knotholes in the raw lumber, their expletives turned the air purple.

I fear there was an element of snobbism in our attitude toward our fellow company members, not only because we thought them as strange as they thought us, but because St. Denis and Shawn had inculcated into their Denishawn Dancers the conviction that our characters and our work placed us among the elite. This was the cause of a personal confrontation at which I can now laugh but which at the time I did not find funny.

One clause in the contract St. Denis and Shawn had signed provided that their dancers must learn the regular chorus numbers so that we would be available as understudies if needed. It was both a sobering and an amusing experience for us, dressed in our customary black wool one-piece tank suits, to line up behind the chorines in their vivid rehearsal togs as we tried to follow their tap steps in our bare feet. Fortunately, we were never called on to expose our ineptitude in public.

When the Miss Miami of the big beauty-pageant scene skipped the show, however, manager Wintz asked me to take her place. I knew she wore a black lace bathing suit and high-heeled black satin slippers, and that all I would have to do was walk down a flight of stairs in the spotlight while twirling a black lace parasol in time to the music. But I fled to Ted Shawn in tears. I could not do such a demeaning thing! Papa, although sympathetic, reminded me of the contract and admitted he was helpless. In desperation, I took my tears directly to Mr. Wintz. That big, rough, tough man was baffled. Why wouldn't I do this? Didn't I know it was kind of an honor?

"Yes, yes, but I can't go on stage in that skimpy costume," I wailed.

"Well, my god!" he roared at me. "You wear a helluva lot less in that *Soaring* thing you dance!"

"I know," I sobbed, "but that's ART!"

After a moment of silence, Mr. Wintz grinned in triumph. "Hey, Jane, honey, I'll betcha you don't know that black lace suit has a *lining!*" We stared at each other across a chasm of absolute incomprehension. Then he sighed. "OK, kid. You don't hafta do it if you don't wanna. Scram." I ran out of the room fast, before he could change his mind.

The very next night *Soaring*, in which I was then dancing Humphrey's center part, stopped the show in Montreal. Mr. Wintz himself signaled for an encore to us and to our pianist in the pit. For the first and only time in that edition of the *Follies*, a number was repeated. And that was my personal high spot as a soi-disant vaudevillian.

Perhaps from the Follies experience and from what I have written earlier it is not strictly accurate to imply that only Ruth St. Denis, Ted Shawn, and their Denishawn Dancers prepared the way for the wonderfully inventive choreography and dance technique we now can see on Broadway, in films, and on television. Denishawn, with all the dignity and devotion to an idea it could command, always had to make money to exist, and the popular theatre helped make this possible. But, unlike Isadora Duncan and Loie Fuller, who left no progeny to carry on their work, Denishawn produced descendents whose contribution to the American musical theatre was significant in ways that have yet to be fully recognized.

For instance, Jack Cole had been a Denishawn pupil, then a member of the last two companies. In 1942 audiences at the *Ziegfeld Follies* applauded his *Hindu Serenade,* which incorporated his special combination of Oriental technique with Occidental movement. In other works Cole introduced what he called "American urban folk," a forerunner of the now familiar modern jazz. He contributed innovative choreography to the Broadway musicals *Alive and Kicking, Kismet* (with Alfred Drake), *Zenda* (1964, with Chita Rivera), and *Man of La Mancha* (1965). In Hollywood he created dances for Marlene Dietrich, Rita Hayworth, and Danny Kaye. His individualistic style was to influence later film choreographers.

After Humphrey and Weidman left Denishawn, their dances were acclaimed outside as well as inside the concert field. Together or separately, they choreographed the Broadway productions *As Thousands Cheer, I'd Rather Be Right, Sing Out, Sweet Land, Life Begins at 8:40,* and *The School for Husbands.* Producer Lee Shubert, for his revue *Americana,* signed Humphrey's serious, religious ensemble work *The Shakers,* unbelievable as this may seem. When he asked Doris to substitute more brightly colored costumes for the traditional dark Shaker garb, she refused with a contemptuous, "Keep your predatory hands off my dances! And I don't suppose you even know what predatory means."

Here Humphrey reflected the integrity St. Denis and Shawn had demonstrated throughout their long and difficult professional lives — and would continue to demonstrate until they died.

Chapter Six
The Orient Tour

IT WOULD REQUIRE SEVERAL books to relate all the details of the tour of
the Far East made by St. Denis, Shawn, and their Denishawn Dancers,
who sailed from Seattle on August 7, 1925, and returned to San Francisco on November 27, 1926. But a single sentence can convey the
significance of that venture: they were the first American company to
present serious Western dance in Japan, China, Burma, India, Ceylon,
Malaya, Java, and the Phillipines, demonstrating a richness of American culture that the people of those countries never suspected existed.

How well Denishawn succeeded in this may be judged by a review
following our opening at the Imperial Theatre in Tokyo. Wrote Baron
Ishimoto in the *Japan Advertiser* of September 23, 1925, "Whenever a
historian tries to write a book on the relations between the U.S. and
Japan, he cannot ignore the coming of the Denishawn Dancers in 1925
to Japan because by their appearance on the stage of Tokyo, the
Japanese attitude towards America in respect to art has been completely
changed. In other words, the historians must pay more attention to
Ruth St. Denis and Ted Shawn than to any other American visitors since
Admiral Perry."

At seventeen, I was the youngest of the eight women dancers and two
men dancers who made up the regular company. Through extreme heat,
under rugged traveling conditions, and surviving a variety of physical
and emotional crises, we absorbed to the limit of our strength the
culture of each country we played. We studied every kind of ethnic
dance, buying suitable costumes from our meager salaries as if each of
us expected to astonish the world with a career that would equal Miss
Ruth's own. Of course such unrealistic ambitions were foredoomed to
failure, but we did shine as an ensemble on our return home for the

1926–1927 United States tour, our new Oriental creations receiving extravagant praise for their brilliance of costume and authenticity. Except for St. Denis and Shawn, however, only Geordie Graham, with her exquisite *Danse Cambodienne*, Doris Humphrey with her Burmese charmer in the *Yein Pwe*, and Anne Douglas as the lead in the Chinese Ballet, achieved distinguished solos.

These works and the balance of the new program that had to be ready for that tour were choreographed during a month's layoff in Singapore, where almost every one of us suffered and rehearsed through a siege of dengue fever. *General Wu Says Farewell to His Wife* was an especially colorful ballet that St. Denis and Shawn had arranged from choreography taught them in Peking by the famous Chinese star, Mei-lan Fan. Douglas, as the heroine, was required to perform a hair-raising dance with two swords. She became the center of twin blades that flashed in constant motion around her turning body, her tours jetés, and small leaps. At the end, with one sword arched over her head and the other held at her waist, she stabs herself and falls dead as the curtain descends. Today Anne remembers, "I never practiced so hard in my life as with those swords. I was supposed to turn and point, and they would waggle. I finally got the trick. But what really scared me was the first time we did the Chinese Ballet in Hong Kong with Chinese people around. The stage hands did laugh some, but it wasn't too bad." It certainly was not "too bad" because Anne's solo always received well-deserved applause.

St. Denis had had no intention of carrying coals to Newcastle by performing her own versions of East Indian dancing in India, but she was persuaded by our impresario to try just one nautch in Rangoon, where a considerable number of Indians would be in the audience. As an introduction to her solo, a trio called the *Dance of the Apsarases* was programmed. Choreographed by St. Denis in 1922, it was a charming little work for three Hindu water nymphs. We wore gossamer silk saris that had been made into full, gold-banded skirts—one blue, one yellow, one green. With our matching cholis, silver anklets and jewelry, and black wigs ending in a long braid, we tripped our flirtatious way onstage. In various formations of lines and circles, all in a bright lighting that suggested sunshine illuminating a temple enclosure, we were supposed to be dancing for the great god Indra. With tiny, bouncing steps and a last smiling glance out at the audience, we tripped offstage as Miss Ruth prepared to make her entrance.

When I had to lead on this trio in Rangoon, it was with real fear and trembling. As I wrote home in January, 1926: "Last night, for the first time in the Orient, we did our Indian numbers. We were scared, and so was Miss Ruth. . . . Well, for the first time since we have done the *Apsarases,* we received applause that slowed Miss Ruth's appearance! And then they yelled for her *Nautch Dance,* then made us repeat the whole big finale. . . . I will never forget that roar of approval as soon as Anne, Edith [James], and I made our entrance and began to do our Western-made dance in our Western-made costumes!"

The pandemonium of applause was repeated throughout our five months in India, because from that moment on we had to include St. Denis Indian solos and ensembles on every program. As Walter Terry was to write in the *Saturday Review* of December 13, 1975, "Ruth St. Denis's non-authentic Indian dances helped reawaken the subcontinent's slumbering dance art and to be at least partly responsible for the renascence of India's respect for its 2,000-year-old dance heritage."

Denishawn Dancers in a publicity photo taken by Brother St. Denis at a deserted temple in Jubbulpore, India, 1926. (Collection Jane Sherman)

All of us who appeared in her East Indian works basked in glory reflected from Miss Ruth's triumph: baskets of orchids, rave newspaper reviews, and the praise of Nobel Prize winner Rabindranath Tagore and other spokesmen for Indian culture. True, it was hinted to us that perhaps this enthusiasm was not entirely what it seemed. The sad fact was that under British rule, the art of the dance had deteriorated to the point where most nautch dancers in India were male or female prostitutes. It was therefore possible that the anti-British, pro-Independence members of the audience were delighted to see white women so demeaning themselves. The truth probably lay somewhere between the peak of admiration and the pit of scorn. We, however, blithely continued to present our material despite some doubts.

This is a good place to mention one aspect of the Orient tour that has largely gone unnoticed, namely the skill involved in the logistics of the unpacking, hanging, and repacking of every show. Our stage manager, Buzz St. Denis, and our one electrician, the superbly unflappable Stanley Frazier, had to oversee this tremendous job in the many towns of the many countries of the Far East in which we appeared. Given the language barrier between them and the local stagehands, the vagaries of electrical voltage and fittings, and the various sizes, shapes, and conditions of the theatres, it is a miracle that they managed to prepare the stage for a performance. Yet our two unsung heroes did this without a hitch, sometimes daily. Brother St. Denis also often ran the show from the wings while he was fully costumed and made up when he had to double as an extra dancer.

I can remember a concert being held up only once, and that through no fault of Stan's or Buzz's. After our luggage had been stowed in the hold of a coast-wise cargo-passenger ship transporting us from Tientsin to Shanghai, a load of loose peanuts was dumped on top of everything. When we reached port several hours behind schedule, the company went straight to the theatre to await the eventual arrival of our freight. Ted Shawn, still in his shipboard clothes, appeared before the curtain to explain the situation to the cream of the city's society that made up the opening-night audience. He gave them a lecture on the history of the dance that continued until every last peanut had been cleared from the ship's hold and our equipment was delivered to the theatre. We gave a very late and exceptionally unpressed program that night.

We were very proud when the Nizam of Hyderabad invited us to perform for him. In 1926 he was said to be the wealthiest man in the world, ruling a large state rich in minerals, and personally owning every one of its coal, iron, gold, and diamond mines. An invitation from him, therefore, was more like a command. At some inconvenience, our schedule was changed to accommodate five performances at Secunderabad, the major city of Hyderabad. The merry month of May found us on a train from Bombay crossing the sweltering Deccan. The following story gives a picture of one of the events that made the Orient tour the amusing, confusing, and bruising experience it was.

We were slightly nervous about dancing for this mighty mogul. He was a Moslem in a predominantly Hindu section of the country, and he had a reputation for being autocratic. Of course we knew he would not slice off our heads with a scimitar if he did not like our dances, as his ancestors might well have done. But what would His Highness think of Shawn's nude *Adonis,* or of Humphrey's sylph clad only in a flesh-colored leotard and dancing with an enormous golden hoop? What would he make of Weidman's *Crapshooter* or our *Boston Fancy?*

Mixed with our trepidation was shamefaced anticipation. Our four months in India to that moment had provided more disillusionment than pleasure; the poverty hurt our hearts, the climate hurt our bodies. Now the syllables Hy-der-a-bad sent visions of sugar plums spinning through our heads. Would we be met at the station by a fleet of Rolls Royces? Be housed in the wing of a palace? Be dined and wined on pheasant *sous cloche* and champagne? Play in a private gem of a theatre, marbled and delicate as a miniature Taj Mahal? While we rattled south in our second-class compartments with their wooden seats—everything dusty and foul-smelling in the 100-degree heat—we worried about the current condition of our evening dresses, should handsome subalterns invite us to after-theatre parties.

We were not met by Rolls Royces, or anything else. As usual, we lugged our bags to the nearest gharry, telling the driver to take us to the hotel where the Nizam's orderly had informed us we were to stay. We badly needed a bath and a rest before going to the theatre to unpack and press our costumes for that night's gala performance, and we looked forward eagerly to the luxuries of modern plumbing and good beds, which this rich man's city would surely provide.

Montgomery's Hotel turned out to be a huge Victorian house. Our large, dusty rooms were furnished with wicker chairs covered in faded, worn chintz and with a pair of sagging beds canopied by mosquito netting. There were neither fans overhead nor screens at the windows, and when we opened a mahogany armoire to hang up our clothes we were assailed by a swarm of mosquitoes that buzzed among us like

maddened wasps. The bathroom was what we had come to expect: a
wash basin, a toilet set like a throne on a platform under its water tank,
a drain in the middle of the slippery gray cement floor, and, in the
darkest corner, an Ali Baba enormous jar filled with lukewarm water.
We always drew small buckets of water from this supply, soaped
ourselves, and rinsed off quickly because we had heard many tales of
snakes lurking in the coolness behind the jars. We discovered that the
hotel food was as English as the ambience: mammoth breakfasts and
teas, with dinners of boiled potatoes, mutton, and cabbage. But after
months of curries, rice, and lemon squash, we almost welcomed this
diet.

After a sponge bath and brief nap, we set off en masse for the theatre.
If the hotel had been a mild disappointment, the theatre was a severe
shock. Set on a blazing sandy plain without a tree in sight, it was a
corrugated-iron walled, thatched-roofed cinema built in 1898 for the
British and Indian troops from the local barracks. Stepping into it from
the outdoor heat was—most literally—stepping into an oven. Faded
British flags graced the back of the stage. Equally faded portraits of
King George and Queen Mary adorned the stage boxes right and left.
Row after row of rickety bamboo chairs supplied audience seating. And
screened by a thin curtain that barely met in the middle was one of the
smallest stages we had ever had to use, its floor grey with dust and
spikey with splinters. Fortunately for our bare feet, Denishawn always
carried a heavy tarpaulin floorcloth that was nailed in place before any
other equipment was unloaded. We discovered there were only two
dressing-rooms at stage level, obviously destined for Miss Ruth and
Papa. The rest of us were banished to rooms that ran around a balcony
on a second floor reached by fragile stairs. We found ourselves laughing
like idiots at this incredible setting for our first "royal command"
performance. Then, mopping the perspiration from brows and bodies,
we did our ironing, laid out our makeup, hung up our costumes, and
went back to the hotel for dinner.

When we returned, we found that our programs for that night were
printed on yellow silk, headed by "In the Gracious Presence of His
Exalted Highness, Lieut-General Asaf Jah, Muzaffar-ul-mulk Wal
Mamalik Nizam-ul-mulk Nizam-ud-Daula, Nawab Mir Sir Osman Ali
Kahn Bahadur, Fateh Jung, Faithful Ally of the British Government,
C.C.S.I., C.B.E., Nizam of Hyderabad." Our romantic hearts began to
beat more swiftly when, in costume, we stood on our balcony overlook-
ing the stage, eager to get our first glimpse of this man of many titles. A

tall, handsome British officer in white dress uniform, a red sash across his chest and red stripes down his spotless trousers, was following closely on the heels of a skinny man with the face of a hawk. He was dressed in plain grey jodhpur breeches with matching long, tight-fitting, high-collared grey coat (Shawn later observed that his shoes needed shining and his socks didn't match). No jewels, no turban, no cloth of gold, no crown; this was the Nizam of Hyderabad.

Accompanied by his resplendent aide-de-camp, he took his place in the right-hand stage box with his English and Indian army officers and bodyguards. Ranged before the box sat fifteen of his sons as stiff and silent as West Point cadets, each wearing a suit exactly like Poppa's only maroon. When Ernestine Day, Anne Douglas, and I took our places for the opening number to Debussy's *Second Arabesque,* we could see a few British ladies dressed in flowered chiffon or lace seated in the front row beside their officer husbands. Behind them were several rows of sun-burned English faces, and behind them a field of black or turbanned heads, all looming above khaki uniforms.

We also saw that black cotton curtains completely shrouded stage box left, converting it into a makeshift purdah. We were later told that thirty of the Nizam's three hundred fifty wives were crammed into that space where they were crudely screened from the sight of men. Tiny flashes, as from fireflies, flickered through the slits that had been cut into the hangings. There, dark eyes peered out at us with as much curiosity as we peered back. We could hear the rustling of silks, the tinkle of belled bracelets, whispers and giggles above the whirr of an electric fan that had been placed in the box to save the poor ladies from suffocation in the unrelenting heat. As our music started, we took a deep breath of air perfumed with sandalwood, patchouli, jasmine, and attar of roses, and began to dance before this strangest of all audiences.

Our concert was received with such enthusiasm that the Nizam himself burst into Miss Ruth's dressing-room to express his appreciation. We were too weary to care. We dressed quickly to walk the long, deserted road back to our hotel. In silence, we followed the fingers of our shadows through moonlight, cool as a waterfall, that spread across the plains, the only sound our footsteps in the thick dust. Once in our rooms, we tucked the mosquito nets around our beds and plunged into sleep.

The next day the Nizam sent cars around to take us on a tour of his capitol. We had heard from a diplomatic attaché that in this city stood a vast storehouse surrounded by a moat and armed guards. Here coffers

Denishawn Dancers in the nautch ballet *In a Bunnia Bazaar.* Left to right, back row: Anne Douglas, Pauline Lawrence, Geordie Graham, Ernestine Day. Center: Jane Sherman. Foreground: Edith James. Photographed in Bombay, India, 1926. (Collection Jane Sherman)

of emeralds, diamonds, and rubies were kept, further protected from theft by cobras that lived among the coffers. These watch-snakes were temporarily collected by a special keeper whenever visitors were brought by His Highness to watch him pour his jewels from bin to bin using an ordinary tin sugar scoop. This fantastic sight was not part of our tour. Instead, we were relegated to a drive around the shabby city, forbidden even to indulge in our favorite sport of bazaar-prowling. The officer in charge claimed it would not be safe for us to enter the markets. It was the only place in India where we found this to be so.

When we returned to the theatre for the next night's concert, stage arrangements had been changed. There was no scenery, just our black velvet cyclorama. The right-hand stage box was crammed with different sons of the household. The left-hand box, sans purdah, was overflowing with young girls in brilliant saris, presumably some of the Nizam's numerous daughters. We watched in amazement as Rolls Royce after Rolls Royce glided up to the open backstage door. When each car came to a halt, attendants holding sheets at arms' length above their heads formed a sort of tunnel through which many more of the Nizam's wives were herded to their seats within a screened-off area directly behind our backdrop.

There they clustered like heavily perfumed, chattering turkeys on a roost, eyes glued to the slits that had been neatly razored in the velvet, as they watched our program from the back. Heavy breathing and muttering continued behind us through all our dances. Heaven alone knows what these cloistered women thought of our behavior as we brazenly capered in near nudity before hundreds of strange men. They were undoubtedly shocked to the soles of their hennaed feet.

This was the pattern followed for the rest of our scheduled performances, until the entire court must have seen at least one program. From time to time, between numbers and in full view of the audience, the resplendent aide-de-camp would march across the stage to thrust bottles of lemon squash or soda through the curtains shielding the wives. Once the Nizam was overseeing this Operation Soft Drink just before a dance was to begin. Late to reach my place, I rushed right past him to reach Miss Ruth's side, but I was ingloriously stopped by the glorious officer who, in an Oxford accent, reprimanded me severely for passing in front of His Exaltedness. Observing this, Miss Ruth gave me a conspiratorial wink as she stifled a giggle.

I was fated to cross His Majesty's path again, this time in a more frightening way. During intermission, I had already dressed for the next dance, which happened to be *Soaring,* in which we wore only skin-tight flesh-colored silk leotards and blonde wigs. The dressing-room was so hot I stepped out onto the balcony for a breath of slightly fresher air. The curtain was closed and the Nizam, as had become his habit, was happily wandering around supervising everything. He was, also as was the habit, closely followed by the handsome aide. Just as I came out onto the balcony, His Highness happened to look up. His eyes bugged wide. The aide looked up. *His* eyes bugged. I am sure they both thought I was nude. When I saw the Nizam make a dash for the stairs, I made a dash back into the dressing-room. I just had time to glimpse the British officer put a restraining hand on the hawklike little ruler's arm to keep him from following me.

Every concert was a wild success, and after each one the Nizam would rush back to tell St. Denis and Shawn how marvellous they and their dancers were. As Papa admits in his book *One Thousand and One Night Stands,* he and Miss Ruth quite naturally expected some tangible recognition of their art that had so impressed the Nizam. After the final show, therefore, they were tingling with anticipation when they saw the aide-de-camp approach carrying a package that was just the size and shape of a jewel box. With another flowery speech of his appreciation, the Nizam motioned the aide to present this small token of his esteem. Hardly had the two men made their formal adieus than Miss Ruth and Papa tore open the wrappings around the box—to find a volume of poems written by the Nizam and inscribed to Ruth St. Denis and Ted Shawn.

That was more than any of the rest of us received from this richest man in the world. We left Hyderabad to finish our tour with yet another disillusionment chalked up against the mysterious East. In 1948 or so, after the company had long been broken up, came the news that the population of Hyderabad had voted to join independent India, and the Nizam had been obliged to renounce nearly his entire fortune when he was removed from power. I am sure neither St. Denis nor Shawn nor any of their Denishawn Dancers shed a tear on his behalf.

Following is the program that was printed on silk when we performed for the Nizam. It is typical of the four completely different ones Denishawn presented throughout the fifteen-month tour of the Orient and on all United States bookings. To modern eyes, accustomed to seeing only a few full-length dances and/or ballets at a concert, these programs may seem inordinately long. It should be kept in mind, however, that St. Denis and Shawn were obeying the custom of the times when audiences, perhaps conditioned by the vaudeville format, expected many brief solos, trios, and ensemble numbers on a single program.

Most of the music visualizations and divertissements listed below lasted no more than four to six minutes, with *Voices of Spring* the longest at ten. I estimate that most of our ballets were from twenty to thirty minutes long. In the Orient, intermissions were customarily extended to allow audiences plenty of time in which to visit the bar for a cooling drink or two.

BRITISH CINEMA
Secunderabad
IN THE GRACIOUS PRESENCE OF
(here followed all his titles, as listed on page 76)
Nizam of Hyderabad
RUTH ST. DENIS with TED SHAWN
and the
Denishawn Dancers

PROGRAMME

MUSIC VISUALIZATIONS
Second Arabesque (Debussy)
Ernestine Day, Anne Douglas, and Jane Sherman
Adagio Pathétique (Godard)
TED SHAWN
Scherzo Waltz (also known as *The Hoop Dance*) (Ilgenfritz)
Doris Humphrey
Album Leaf and Prelude (Scriabin)
Ernestine Day and Charles Weidman
De Lachau Waltz
Doris Humphrey with Anne Douglas, Geordie Graham, Edith James, and Jane Sherman
Waltz (Op. 33 #15, Brahms), *Liebestraum* (Liszt)
RUTH ST. DENIS
Voices of Spring (also known as *La Primavera*) (Strauss)
Pictorial inspiration from Botticelli's Painting *Primavera,* in Florence. Doris Humphrey, Anne Douglas, Geordie Graham, Ernestine Day, Edith James, Jane Sherman, Charles Weidman, and George Steares

INTERMISSION

Cuadro Flamenco
A Spanish Gypsy Dance Scene

Characters

Cuadro Flamenco: Anne Douglas, Geordie Graham, Ernestine Day, Doris Humphrey, and Charles Weidman

Flower Sellers: Edith James, Jane Sherman, and Mary Howry
Sevillanos: George Steares and B. St. Denis
Lalanda, a famous Matador: TED SHAWN
La Macarena, a dancer, the idol of all Sevilla: RUTH ST. DENIS

INTERMISSION

DIVERTISSEMENTS
Japanese Flower Arrangement (Robert Hood Bowers)
RUTH ST. DENIS
Garland Plastique (Schubert)
Anne Douglas, Ernestine Day, Jane Sherman, Geordie Graham, and Edith James
American Sketches
>   *Invocation to the Thunderbird* (Sousa)
>   TED SHAWN
>   *A Creole Belle* (also known as *Pasquinade*) (Gottschalk)
>   Doris Humphrey
>   *The Crapshooter* (Eastwood Lane)
>   Charles Weidman
>   *Around the Hall in Texas* (Lane)
>   Anne Douglas and TED SHAWN
>   *A Gringo Tango* (Lane)
>   Ernestine Day and TED SHAWN
>   *The Legend of Pelée, Hawaiian Volcano Goddess* (Vaughan)
>   RUTH ST. DENIS
>   *Boston Fancy: 1854* (Lane)
>   TED SHAWN and Doris Humphrey, Charles Weidman and Pauline Lawrence, B. St. Denis and Jane Sherman, Geordie Graham and George Steares

Dance of the Apsarases (Crist)
Anne Douglas, Edith James, and Jane Sherman
Nautch (Cadman)
RUTH ST. DENIS and Denishawn Dancers

INTERMISSION

SUITE OF DANCES INSPIRED BY THE ART FORMS OF ANCIENT EGYPT
(Walter Meyrowitz and L. Halvorsen)
Tillers of the Soil
RUTH ST. DENIS and TED SHAWN
Thoth and Horus
Charles Weidman and George Steares
Dance of the Tambourines
Doris Humphrey with Denishawn Dancers
Dance of the Rebirth
RUTH ST. DENIS and TED SHAWN

Costumes designed by Ruth St. Denis, Ted Shawn, and Pearl Wheeler, and executed in the Denishawn School, 327 West 28th St., New York City, U.S.A.

New numbers were added to our programs as they were created en route while we were in the Orient. The intention was to give to the people of the Far East as varied a picture as possible of our dance culture. This I think St. Denis and Shawn accomplished, to judge by critical and audience response to works like *Boston Fancy,* which often had to be encored, Shawn's Amerind solos, and St. Denis's *Liebestraum.* Since St. Denis with her East Indian creations also unquestionably stimulated the Indians' appreciation of their own dance art, it might be said that this tour was the first of the many successful cultural exchanges that have since been instigated between the United States and other nations of the world.

Baron Ishimoto, whose article was quoted at the beginning of this chapter, concluded with a prescient thought:

It is natural for Japanese to look on America as being busy transplanting various art objects from the old mother countries of Europe, and to conclude that nothing new or creative can be found in the land of automobiles and the radio. Two evenings at the Imperial Theatre [Tokyo] were enough to revolutionize our opinion towards American art. The Denishawn Dancers convinced the Japanese audiences that America is now creating its own art, and *moreover it has something very suggestive of the future* (emphasis added).

Chapter Seven

The Great Independents: Graham, Horst, Humphrey, Lawrence, and Weidman

As IF DRAWN BY a pair of powerful magnets, they came to Ruth St. Denis and Ted Shawn almost at the same time. Martha Graham enrolled in the school in 1916. Louis Horst was employed as a pianist for a Denishawn vaudeville and concert tour that same year. Doris Humphrey traveled from Illinois to study teaching in 1917. Pauline Lawrence came as a pianist right out of high school in 1917, and Charles Weidman became a Denishawn pupil in 1919. Roughly a decade later, Graham, Humphrey, and Weidman had left Denishawn to present independent concerts of their own choreography. Horst participated in the new movement as composer, musical director, and choreographic advisor par excellence. Lawrence contributed her immeasurable talents as pianist, costume designer, and manager.

Martha Graham, the first of the greats to leave the fold, had been the earliest of them to arrive. In 1911, when she was seventeen, her father had taken her to see St. Denis in Los Angeles. It was the first dance performance she had ever seen. (Coincidentally, her experience occurred only one month after the fateful moment when Ted Shawn first saw St. Denis in Denver.) As Don McDonagh writes in his biography of Graham, it was then that ". . . perhaps half unconsciously herself, she began to prepare to be a dancer. The rest of her life was to be spent trying to realize in her own person the vision that she saw in Ruth St. Denis."

As has been noted, when Graham joined her classes in 1916, St. Denis saw no corresponding vision in the twenty-two-year-old pupil whom she considered too old to begin to learn serious dancing. She found Graham's dark-eyed, high-cheek-boned face, and her then dumpy figure far from the Denishawn ideal. It was Shawn who recognized determination that equaled his own, and after he saw Graham do the class dance *Serenata Morisca* with such fire and abandon that sparks seemed to fly, he took her under his wing. He gave her private lessons without charge, and when he had to go out on the road, assigned her the responsibility of teaching night classes to adult beginners in his small Los Angeles school. Within a short time, although Graham herself was still learning her craft, she became a member of his teaching staff.

Shawn, however, had not forgotten her ability to project a dance, and he had no intention of losing a promising performer to the routine of a studio. When he was asked to create a vaudeville act to succeed his popular *Julnar of the Sea,* he choreographed the Aztec ballet *Xochitl* for his exotic, temperamental, and talented pupil. After touring in this with Weidman, Graham remained a Denishawn Dancer for three years of cross-country tours, performing solos and duets with Shawn and Weidman, as well as ensemble numbers. It is by now well known that when the Broadway producer John Murray Anderson saw Graham dance *Serenata Morisca* during the 1922–1923 Daniel Mayer United States tour, he urged her to join the cast of his *Greenwich Village Follies.* So at age twenty-nine Graham left Denishawn to take her first independent dance step.

After two seasons, she came to feel that dancing in the *Follies* condemned her to the status of mere entertainer and that unless she could free herself from revue work as she had freed herself from Denishawn, she would not be able to develop as a creative dancer. Fortunately, at that precise time she was offered a teaching position at the Eastman School of Dance and Dramatic Action in Rochester, New York. This came about as the result of a combination of circumstances: George Eastman, head of the Kodak Company, had already founded his Eastman School of Music. He wanted to expand this to include a department in the staging of opera productions. As organizer of this department he engaged Rouben Mamoulian, a European director. Mamoulian had been greatly impressed by Graham when he saw her with the Denishawn Company during their concert at the Eastman Theatre in Rochester on November 1, 1922. He had seen her again in the second year of the *Greenwich Village Follies,* and now, when he needed someone to run the Department of Dance at the new Eastman institution, he asked Graham to share this responsibility with Esther Gustafson. Although, like St. Denis, Graham did not enjoy teaching, she accepted the post, recognizing it as an opportunity to escape from Broadway and begin the work of becoming the serious artist she intended to be.

Graham was greatly helped in her initial creative efforts by the emotional and musical support given her by Louis Horst. He had played for her earliest Denishawn classes and throughout the tours, during one of which they formed a close association that was to last for twenty years.

When St. Denis and Shawn planned their Orient tour, they of course expected Horst to go with them, but he declined, preferring instead to study in Vienna because he felt he needed to work on his own music. (St. Denis was later to say, sadly, "When Louis left us in 1925, that was the real beginning of the disintegration of Denishawn.") On his return to the States he joined Graham. As McDonagh notes, "Horst was fond of saying that an artist, like a plant, needs a wall to grow against: he became Graham's wall. He believed in her talent and encouraged her to develop it. He provided her with sound information about music and art. . . . And, in addition to being her intellectual sounding board, he was her emotional shelter."

For her first independent concert on April 18, 1926, at the 48th Street Theatre in New York City, they evolved a program of solos for herself and trios for three young women who had been Graham's pupils at the Eastman School. With its emphasis on the theatrical, the skilled use of lighting, and Horst's choice of music, it was a program that clearly showed the Denishawn influence. This could be seen in Graham's dependence on costumes for effect; in her use of props, in the sense that the *Soaring* veil had been a prop; in her wigs, her scarves, her careful attention to makeup. (Even beneath her later intensely personal creations, the Denishawn roots could be perceived in her imaginative practical sets and her dramatic, sculptural handling of fabrics.)

Graham had not yet developed her technique of contraction and release, the Delsartean inspiration for which she had learned from Shawn. She had not yet fully explored the use of the floor to strengthen the torso, a technique that had been impressed upon her by Ronny Johansson, the Swedish modern dancer she had first seen at the Denishawn studio. (Under the pseudonym of Ronnie Joyce, this fine artist had earned her living for almost a year as a Denishawn Dancer featured in the *Ziegfeld Follies* road company in 1927– 1928.) Nor had Graham freed herself from the Oriental spirit that had so uplifted her in St. Denis. The "long underwear" period of clenched fists, angular arms, slicked-back hair, and grim face was yet to come.

In her first program, the audience saw Graham and her three student dancers in a *Chorale* to music by César Franck. Graham, wearing a long, blonde, pig-tailed wig, interpreted Debussy's *The Maid with the Flaxen Hair,* and three figures floated gracefully to that same composer's *First Arabesque* (choreographed as a solo by St. Denis in 1919). Graham appeared as a Tanagra figurine accompanied by Erik Satie's avant garde melodies, then as a Florentine Madonna, and finally as a de Falla *Gypsy* from which, of all her solos, emerged the strongest indication of the direction she would eventually take. The concert earned a brief review in the *New York Times,* which reported, "Martha Graham gave an evening of interpretive dance to modern music," praising her for her beautiful images and her lyrical talent but (who today would believe it?) mildly chastising her for her "lack of power"!

My mother was in that first audience, responding, as she wrote me in the Orient, with enthusiasm to the emotionally moving works. She sent me a copy of the program. When I showed it to Geordie, she burst into tears at sight of a photograph of her sister, exclaiming, "Oh! But she looks so *sad!*" We consoled her with our conviction that the concert must have been wonderful.

A curious observation might be made about that 1926 concert. In using only female dancers, Graham was following the tradition of the Ruth St. Denis Concert Dancers. Both before and after her marriage to Shawn, St. Denis had toured either as a soloist or with a group consisting only of young women. Humphrey appeared with this group, but Graham had not. All Denishawn programs, however, included one or two male dancers in addition to Shawn himself. It would be interesting to know if Graham's elimination of the male element was necessitated by the lack of suitable men dancers, or by her no doubt unconscious imitation of St. Denis, whom she always continued to admire deeply. Or was it, as McDonagh suggests, because women were all that her creative objectives of the moment needed?

Even if the last were true, it still seems strange when one considers that, in addition to ensembles, she had danced duets with men from her earliest stage appearances with Charles Weidman in *Xochitl.* During a tour without St. Denis in 1921, she danced the duos *Malagueña* and the Egyptian *Dance of Rebirth,* as well as *Xochitl* with Shawn and an *Arabic Duet* with Weidman. In 1922 in London she was Shawn's partner in a *Spanish Suite* and again in *Xochitl*. In the 1922–1923 Mayer tour of the United States she danced with Weidman in the Javanese *Princess and the Demon,* and with Shawn in the enduring *Xochitl*. Yet, except for a single concert in Rochester, New York, in 1926, it was not until the late 1930s that Graham incorporated into her works the dramatic tension inherent in a male-female encounter. It was not until 1929 that she could gather a permanent company to present *Heretic,* the first of her great creations for an ensemble. What followed produced a chapter unequaled in the American theatre.

The lack of a male presence and the emphasis on solo rather than group work represent two significant differences between the early concerts of the independents. When Doris Humphrey presented her first program after leaving Denishawn, it was, of course, in partnership with Charles Weidman, and its most important dances had been choreographed for ensembles. Despite their long years of friendship, the inclusion of Weidman as dancer-choreographer was unusual because in all her years with Denishawn, Humphrey had never danced with either Shawn or Weidman except in ballets or smaller group works. (Weidman, however, had been assigned several duets with Graham, Anne Douglas, Ruth Austin, and Ernestine Day.) From 1918 when she appeared on a vaudeville tour with Ruth St. Denis and three other young women, until the second Mayer tour of 1923–1924, Humphrey had performed without any male dancers even present in the group.

Humphrey, a year younger than Graham, had come to Denishawn a year later. St. Denis (as she had not discerned in the neophyte Graham) at once recognized the talents of the young woman from Illinois who had already been teaching dance for several years. Humphrey was slim, violet-eyed, and had reddish hair. She moved with a delicacy of strength that suited the St. Denis ideal. Despite her considerable previous dance experience, Humphrey approached her first private lessons with Miss Ruth with excitement tinged by apprehension. After having watched her dance for about a half an hour, St. Denis asked her, "What do you do?" To which Doris replied, "I teach." As Humphrey later recorded in her autobiography, *An Artist First,* Miss Ruth then said, "'You shouldn't be teaching. You should be dancing.' I could hardly believe my ears. This is what I had been waiting to hear for five long years." Thus began an association that ended only when Humphrey, Weidman, and Lawrence left Denishawn to form their own school and company.

Since I was part of that company and since I had earlier studied or worked with all three for at least four years, while I had known Martha only at a distance, I can report on the first Humphrey-Weidman concert in greater detail than I could on Graham's. When Humphrey and Weidman took a final bow with their band of sixteen dancers at the end of their performance on October 28, 1928, they could not have known that they had made dance history with the first presentation of an American modern ensemble.

Humphrey's greatest concern had been to keep that ensemble together. Unlike Graham at this period of their respective developments, Doris found it restrictive to choreograph only solos. "I like groups of people so much better—but the people are not so good, so there we are," she said. Using her not-so-good people, she nevertheless forged ahead to create three memorable ensemble dances. Her student-performers were devoted and hard-working, but most of them had had precious little time in which to absorb her unfamiliar technique or rehearse her numbers. They had been recruited from Denishawn classes at the school where Humphrey and Weidman taught in 1927–1928 while St. Denis and Shawn, with nine members of their company, were on the road with the *Ziegfeld Follies*.

The break with Denishawn, inevitable as it may seem in hindsight, came as a shock as much to Humphrey, Weidman, and Lawrence as to Miss Ruth and Papa. When Doris and Charles opened their own school at 9 East 59th Street in New York shortly thereafter, nearly every dancer in their original group decided to leave the Denishawn school to study and perform with them. Eleanor King and Gertrude Shurr were among this group, and Geordie Graham and I, from the Denishawn Company, joined them. Contrary to allegations that we had been "kidnapped," we came to Humphrey-Weidman of our own free will. Humphrey had been fearful, however, writing home, "I must guard against an insidious attack on the group because that is where I live and I have sixteen vulnerable spots. I have stated clearly to them the truth as I see it, and most of all, the principle that it is greater to adhere to that truth than to any one person or institution and then they must judge for themselves." We did judge for ourselves.

I, for one (and I suspect Geordie Graham as well) found my loyalties to Denishawn strained by the conflict I sensed between the unrealistic aims of St. Denis and the materialistic ambitions of Shawn in their building of what they called Greater Denishawn. Therefore despite their persistent urging that I rejoin them after I had rested from the *Follies* tour, I could not in all honesty do so. Since I also wanted to be part of the new dance movement, I enrolled in the Humphrey-Weidman School and soon found myself part of their company.

Most of the members of that company had to earn a living as typists or whatever, taking class in the evening and rehearsing late into the night. Humphrey and Weidman taught other classes during the day. As we jumped, turned, stamped, fell, and rose to jump again on the cold brown linoleum of the studio floor to Lawrence's tireless playing, we were scarcely history-making material. Humphrey, with her vision of what her dances should be, must have observed our brave efforts with despair, yet she never by word or gesture showed impatience with us as, through sheer courage and determination, she molded her group into a presentable unit. It was a revelation to expand Denishawn technique into the new ways of movement that Doris was exploring. It was also a privilege to watch two maturing artists emerge from tradition into original works, even as Miss Ruth and Papa had done before them.

Two of the three ensemble numbers on the Humphrey-Weidman premiere program, *Water Study* and the *Grieg piano concerto in A minor*, might be seen to have roots in earlier Humphrey choreography. The first traces back to *Sonata Tragica* created with St. Denis in 1923, undoubtedly the first musicless dance widely performed in public in America. The dance to Grieg's concerto finds its ancestry in the 1919 *Sonata Pathétique*, also choreographed by Humphrey with St. Denis (see pps. 48–49). But the third ensemble piece, *Color Harmony*, shows no signs of Denishawn. As Humphrey wrote, "There may have been other abstract ballets done in America, but I've never seen one—and I'm quite proud of it."

As well she might have been. Here she first used music specifically written to her idea. This was composed by Clifford Vaughan. The movement was projected, then the musical form followed. As in the *Concerto*, Humphrey used her famous setting of boxes as off-center steps before tall angled screens that reflected shafts of light from the wings. Against this background moved four dancers in dark red, three in scarlet, four in green, four in purple, and one in violet. Some wore leotards, some long-sleeved, close-fitting short jersey tunics, and the three in scarlet had narrow strips of material wound like flames around their bare arms. Heads were turbaned in colored jersey that matched the tunics. Weidman as the central dancer was costumed in a white, long-sleeved silk jersey leotard. He wore a stiff white wig that flared like brief streaks of lightning straight back from his forehead.

Humphrey's program note explains the dance:

Each of the three primary [*sic*] colors moves according to its own being: the red is both sensual and scintillating, the green moves soothingly, the purple is rich, threaded by an aspiring violet. As each color follows its own course, it is inevitably flung against another, and as each collision occurs, a new color suddenly emerges. The confusion becomes greater and rapidly draws toward chaos and death. Through the maelstrom appears a silver light symbolic of controlling intelligence [Weidman] which draws all the flaming colors into the rhythmic harmony of its own essence.

After Weidman disciplines the colors into their separate categories to form different patterns, he leads them into a cohesive design that closes the dance. He stands at the top of a flight of steps facing into a bright spotlight from stage left, his commanding figure a silver apex exemplifying the creative principle. Descending from this apex, the colors spread down the stairs from violet through green through red and scarlet to end in a peacocklike tail of purple flat on the floor.

Humphrey wrote of *Color Harmony*'s first performance that "People are simply stunned—they said they had never seen anything like it." One critic called it a dance masterpiece, and John Martin said it constituted the beginning of the modern dance ensemble in America. Unbeknownst to Humphrey and Weidman, St. Denis had attended the concert at the Civic Repertory Theatre. Although she could not bring herself to go backstage afterward, she did send Doris a note to say that *Color Harmony* was "stupendous." About that generous act Doris observed, "It is the great part of Miss Ruth who could do this."

An equal if different impact on the audience was made by the first movement of the Grieg piano concerto, the earliest of Humphrey's ensemble numbers created independently of Denishawn. She called it ". . . a great satisfaction after all the whipped cream and applesauce of other days." There was little whipped cream and no applesauce in this composition. Lighted principally from the wings, a large platform reached by two steps stood against old-gold screen panels. Humphrey and her fourteen dancers wore identical rust-colored long-sleeved, high-necked short silk jersey tunics, and their heads were bare.

Concerto is loosely structured as an antiphon wherein Humphrey's solo figure represents the piano melodies and the group represents the orchestral responses. Like *Sonata Pathétique*, it has no specific story. Also similarly, its formations suggest a small army involved in a vague battle with commander and soldiers aligned against the enemy at times, and at other times the rank and file contending against their soloist leader. It was as exciting to dance as it must have been to watch, and it aroused enthusiasm at every performance. As Doris reported after its

Doris Humphrey, with the first Humphrey-Weidman Company, in the opening movement of the *Grieg Piano Concerto in A minor,* allegro marcato. Photographed in performance at the Civic Repertory Theatre, New York, October 28, 1928. Photo by Van Damm. (Collection Jane Sherman)

premiere, "Both we and the audience at the end were at such a pitch of excitement everybody wanted to yell and did. Imagine the thrill of having a whole house crying 'bravo!'—not once but every time the curtain went up [for the bows]."

The reception given *Water Study* was even more astonishing because it must surely have seemed the strangest dance on the entire program. Many have seen it since in revivals, but imagine the amazement of that 1928 audience when the curtain rose on four rows of dancers, four to each row, who are lying prone on the stage in a blue-green light and who then begin to move in absolute silence. The back row arches to knees, backs rounded, heads down, then subsides into the next row which also slowly arches and subsides into the second row and so into the row nearest the footlights. As these dancers unfold down flat, their arms reach out in a circular movement on the floor, fingers scrabbling like wavelets on sand. Immediately the back row arches again, and the beautiful, quiet opening is repeated.

When the rows break, the movements of the ensemble swell into ebb and flow, into larger waves then into solid masses crashing against each other. The pounding feet and audible panting of sixteen dancers became part of the element. To this day I do not comprehend how Doris achieved this unanimity of intent without the beat of music. There was a sense of gigantic "breathing" as each body imparted its own motion, its own rhythm, to the others, and all together realized a unity that resembled the sea. Humphrey's program note explains that "probably the thing that distinguishes musical rhythm from other rhythms is the measured time beat, so this has been eliminated from the *Water Study* and the rhythm flows in natural phrases instead of cerebral measures. There is no count to hold the dancers together in the very slow opening rhythm, only the feel of the wave length that curves the backs of the group."

At the time of its premiere, Mary Watkins wrote, "Real genius has gone into the creating of this." Clive Barnes, reviewing a 1973 revival, said that *Water Study* went beyond mimicry to "stand alone as a graphic poem to the beauty of the human body in movement."

What were they like, the "unholy three" who made possible that first performance of the Humphrey-Weidman Company? I answer as one who knew them only at the beginning of their independent careers. Long before I met her, Doris was the glamorous dancer who was part of my family mythology. Her father, as a college student, was such a close friend of my grandfather's that when the first Sherman son, my father, was born thirteen years before Doris, he was named Horace Humphrey after his godfather. I knew Doris first as a person when at age sixteen, I was an advanced student at the Denishawn School in Carnegie Hall. She was a strict and inspiring teacher, but not a severe one. I held her in such awe that I could seldom speak to her. Later I knew her as rehearsal mistress for the Denishawn Dancers, coworker in ensemble numbers, and fellow traveler.

Even as a child she was never pretty in the baby-doll sense, but she was beautiful onstage. She never let down, whether dancing her own solos or one of the many minor roles assigned her in a boring ballet alongside the rest of us. Although she had toured with Miss Ruth, Papa, and some of the older dancers for many years, she usually remained aloof from everyone except Weidman and Lawrence, as if her limited physical strength reduced her capacity for friendship to a selected few. With her unfailing tact, she never intruded into the affairs of others and she never gossiped.

Some may have thought her cold, but Doris could and did openly express anger at artistic or financial injustice when crossing swords with Shawn. She could and did flee in hysterics down a hotel hall to escape from an overly demanding mother. She could and did take a homesick youngster into her own room to nurse her through dengue fever in Singapore. She could and did attract many a charming and wealthy man in the Far East, at least one of whom she seriously considered marrying. (Later, in the States, she did marry and have a son.) Perhaps most important, she could and did dance with a fire and abandon that entranced audiences.

Almost from the start of her relationship with Denishawn, Humphrey had demonstrated a talent for choreography in addition to her obvious performing and pedagogic abilities. She soon became the only Denishawner to create solo and group dances that were regularly presented on programs with works by St. Denis and Shawn. Were there hints of her later modern technique in those early Denishawn creations? Looking back, I believe two of the least known of the ten dances she choreographed in that period clearly presage the Humphrey that was to come. The first of these was her 1919 *Bourrée,* to Bach's Partita, Suite no. 1 in B minor for violin. Dressed in a short scarlet satin tunic, she gave physical shape to the music's rubatos, repetitions, accelerandos, and accents that aroused the identical emotion of controlled inevitability that the composition itself aroused. All movements rose from disciplined, pointed, bare toes and strong legs, and all gestures were powerful and forthright, even when made with rounded arms and graceful hands. Here Humphrey's confidence, projection, experiments with balance, and perceptive musicality were present in embryo. Her achievement is all the more remarkable when one considers that Doris had been with Denishawn only three years when she created this original dance that was so different from any she had previously performed.

Whims, choreographed in 1926 for herself, Weidman, and five young women, showed Humphrey and Weidman working together in a way that pointed significantly toward the future. It was the closest they had yet come to a duo. Done to Schumann's *Grillen,* it was a strange experimental dance. To those of us on whom she worked out her ideas, its non-ethnic simplicity was a welcome relief from the intricacies of Oriental techniques. As the title indicates, the dance reflected changing moods; however, these were the caprices of children rather than adults. All of us wore simple blue tunics, and bright orange sandals that had been made to order for us in Shanghai. They were of leather, with firm soles and low heels. To don any kind of footwear for a music visualization represented shocking defiance of Denishawn tradition, but I think Doris demanded this anomaly, these props, if you will, so as to emphasize the universal, noisy, and often rowdy antics of children at play.

With Doris in the lead, the six female dancers are pulled onstage by Weidman in a close-knit group clasping hands. Their steps, pounded out on the sandal soles, emphasize the opening piano phrase of seven loud staccato chords. At the end of this phrase, the six dancers swiftly reverse their weight to fling themselves into an extreme backbend, knees flexed, hands still gripped, as they impel Weidman backward toward them. This visible and audible tug-of-war is repeated when Weidman again pulls the group across the stage as if by his own irresistible power.

The boisterous mood of the entrance alters with the mood of the next musical theme. The ensemble breaks into smiling, relaxed pairs and trios, each with its own games, its own steps. These patterns shift with the musical patterns to weave an impression of children as they drift from organized team play into their own dream worlds and back again. At the end, the strenuous tug-of-war resumes when the group re-forms and Weidman pulls them across stage to exit.

Although Doris reported after its premiere in Los Angeles on December 6, 1926, that "It went most comfortably well," it always seemed to me that audiences were as puzzled by the dance's unfamiliar technique and ambiguous meaning as were the performers. Whatever the reasons, *Whims* never received the acclaim that other Humphrey creations invariably evoked.

My memories of Weidman are less vivid than of Humphrey because, although I studied, rehearsed, and danced with him for the same length of time as I did with Doris, he was more remote than she. Where Humphrey wore an armor of distance to hold intimacy at bay, he carried a shield of wit that hid his frustrations or sorrows. He seemed determined always to appear light-hearted, almost flippant, but he was earnest about his dancing. I cannot recall his ever kidding around onstage, even when tempted, like the rest of us, by the ennui of deadly repetition to do so. Offstage, his mimicry of Miss Ruth and Papa in certain aspects of their dancing could be hilariously disrespectful, but his often biting comic comment was as much appreciated by them as by us.

On the Orient tour, Charles was noticeably protective of Doris, holding a paper parasol to screen her from the blazing Indian sun, unpacking her costumes, carrying her purchases when they shopped, and, more significantly, cushioning her as best he could against the strain of her relationship with her mother. (It is interesting to note en passant that Humphrey shared with St. Denis the problem of a domineering mother. This may well have been an unspoken bond between the two artists.)

It was Shawn who immediately perceived Weidman's great gift for pantomime when the young Nebraskan came to the Denishawn school, and he capitalized on this gift in the early dances he choreographed specifically for Charles, notably *The Crapshooter* and *Danse Americaine*. In the years from 1920 to 1927 when Weidman was with the Denishawn company, he danced the lead in *Xochitl* and six solos, all created by Shawn.

Except for roles in ballets, St. Denis never choreographed a solo for Weidman, although she admired his work, particularly in the comic-poignant *Pierrot Forlorn,* the first solo created by Shawn for Charles. Conventionally costumed for the picture of Pierrot serenading his love to no avail and danced to rather nondescript music, it was nevertheless a pantomime gem. Originally, Weidman "played" on a long-necked banjolike instrument. When, because of lack of space, this prop had to be discarded for the Orient tour, Charles used his ragged, drooping sleeves with which to pantomime the plucking of strings. Whenever St. Denis was free to do so, she always came to the wings to watch him do this dance.

Pierrot Forlorn may have been the ancestor of Weidman's trio set to Debussy's music, *Minstrels,* and programmed on the first Humphrey-Weidman concert. There is little doubt that his *Japanese Actor (XVII*

Century) to Horst's music had Denishawn predecessors. In the early 1920s, as part of a Japanese suite, Shawn created *Japanese Servant with Parasol* and *Coolie Dance,* both of which Weidman performed. Of course, he had watched Shawn's own *Japanese Spear Dance* so often he could have done it himself, and in 1926 Shawn gave Charles the important role of Mountain God in the Kabuki dance-drama called *Momiji-Gari.* To prepare for this part Weidman had to know how to apply the fearful and fearfully complicated makeup and costume required. This he learned directly from the famous actor-dancer Koshiro Matsumoto in Tokyo, an experience that probably determined the shape and content of his 1928 Japanese actor solo.

Although Weidman was to become best known for his wonderfully inventive comic pieces *Flickers, Fables of our Times,* and *Daddy Was a Fireman,* he had a sober side that was to find expression in works such as *Lynchtown.* Two of his numbers on the first Humphrey-Weidman program reflected this seriousness in ways that indicated Denishawn influence. His Debussy *Cathédrale Engloutie* seemed based on St. Denis's music visualization theories. His whole body was engulfed in a weird olive-green costume that suggested granite encrusted with barnacles. Made of a stiff material, it hung straight down from exaggerated square shoulders. Even thus encumbered, he indicated with a truly moving quality the surge of sea depths, the rising and sinking of the submerged structure, and the tolling of underwater bells. His duet with Humphrey to the *Scriabin Étude* (opus 8, no. 12) in its musicality and modern movements reminded one forcibly of the Scriabin *Album Leaf and Prelude* created in 1924 by Shawn and danced by Weidman first with Ruth Austin and then Ernestine Day.

Although Weidman's dances on this first program demonstrated a strength and originality that had not been previously emphasized in his Denishawn works, it is safe to say that he remained at this time more deeply under the Denishawn influence than did Humphrey. In his later years, the pantomime genius discovered and developed by Shawn provided a powerful basis for his most important creations. As John Martin wrote in 1963, however, "Charles's is by no means realistic pantomime when he gets through with it, for he takes actual gesture and reduces it to its very essence as movement. . . . [he] has a wonderful gift for observing and visualizing the vagaries of men and manners." This astute evaluation could have correctly been made of the young Weidman forty years earlier.

Charles Weidman in *Quest,* a post-Denishawn dance. Photo, Bouchard. (Collection Jane Sherman)

What of Pauline Lawrence at that time? Because she was closer to us than Doris or Charles in rehearsing and performing ensemble dances, sharing dressing-rooms and train compartments, and participating in parties and our bazaar prowling in the Orient, I found her personality more accessible. P'line, as Weidman had nicknamed her, was worldly and even-tempered, shrewd and funny, as sharp-tongued, witty, and perceptive as he but seldom expressing her observations with malice. She was not much older than several of the other Denishawn Dancers, yet she seemed maternal, possibly because she was inclined to plumpness that lent maturity. Like Weidman, she was protective of Humphrey's well-being.

A dancer manquée, P'line appeared in many group numbers where great talent was not essential, but her true gift was as a musician. With her small, fine-boned hands and endless patience she was a deft, indefatigable pianist for class or rehearsal. I could not, when I knew her, suspect that in addition to her musical skills she would be capable of contributing so much more to the Humphrey-Weidman evolution. She showed no interest then in the costume designing that was later to flower into real creativity, and there were certainly no opportunities for her to learn how to manage the complicated financial and booking problems of an impresario, as she was later to do with real brilliance not only for Doris and Charles but for her future husband, José Limón, and his company. It must have been true in those Denishawn days that even as Humphrey and Weidman were subconsciously developing their new technique, pedagogy, and choreography, Lawrence was nurturing within herself those latent abilities that were to make possible the realization of the triumvirate's aims during the next seventeen years.

Surely only the fortunate combination of the exceptional talents and efforts of all three of these people made possible their accomplishments within that year and a half from April 1927 to October 1928: teaching, creating major works, giving two concerts, breaking with Denishawn, founding a school of their own, and mounting that epochal first independent program. Looking back, it in no way belittles Doris to perceive that in the beginning Charles and P'line were two crutches upon whom she relied to take her first steps. Nor does it belittle Charles and P'line to conclude that Doris was the prime creative force behind the drive for independence from Denishawn, and the prime teaching force to move young dancers along the path of independence from her. As José Limón wrote, "In Doris Humphrey I found a master who knew that every dancer, being an individual, was an instrument unique and distinct from any other, and that in consequence this dancer must ultimately find his own dance, as she had found hers"—and as Charles found his.

This, then, is how a contemporary remembers the Humphrey, Weidman, and Lawrence of more than fifty years ago. In my young eyes they and Graham and Horst were magnificent. I believe they will remain magnificent as long as the history of American dance is read and evaluated. They helped write that history, not alone through their great and original performing and choreography, but through their pupils and their pupils' pupils. Among those influential dancers too numerous to list in toto, Weidman had taught Sybil Shearer, Eleanor King, William Bales, and Jack Cole. Humphrey had taught José Limón, Pauline Koner, Ruth Currier, and Katherine Litz. Graham had taught Anna Sokolow, Merce Cunningham, May O'Donnell, Pearl Lang, Erik Hawkins, Paul Taylor, Daniel Nagrin, and Sophie Maslow. Jane Dudley had studied with Graham and with Horst, while Alwin Nikolais had been a pupil of Graham, Humphrey, Weidman, and Horst.

The chain now has hundreds of links of different shapes and values, but every one connects in a long line reaching straight back to Ruth St. Denis and Ted Shawn in a process that would have made those two innovators justifiably proud. And every one, the now famous and the yet unknown, will add another link to that chain for as long as mankind continues to dance.

Chapter Eight
On Their Own

BY 1932 A RECONCILIATION of the personal differences between Ruth
St. Denis and Ted Shawn became impossible, and since the Orient tour
their professional aims had diverged even more widely than they had in
the past. At age forty-seven, Miss Ruth felt that after the many years of
unrelenting performing, traveling, and teaching she had to have a rest
period in which to recoup her creative powers, especially after the long
nightmare of the *Follies* tour. She had hoped to achieve this time for
self-regeneration within the walls of the new Denishawn House that
had been built with the hard-earned money from that tour. Shawn, on
the other hand, saw that they must keep working to keep living.

It was during the *Follies* experience that the personal differences
between the two reached an impasse. Although each tried bravely to
share with the other the responsibility to realize their plans for Greater
Denishawn, their emotional lives had suffered an irrevocable sea
change.

This sad truth was reflected in their profession. New choreography
frequently lacked inspiration. Bookings, affected by the Great Depression, became fewer and fewer. The grandiose schemes for Denishawn
House and School failed to materialize, and the establishment was soon
a financial burden that could not be maintained. Faced with foreclosure
on their dream, St. Denis and Shawn reluctantly, with mutual love and
respect, accepted foreclosure on their private lives as well. Their separation, while permanent, was never bitter nor did it ever lead to divorce.

After the financial debacle, Miss Ruth was homeless and penniless
except for a small income from the annuity Shawn had had the foresight

to buy for her from their *Follies* income. She moved to a simple loft in New York City that had been offered to her rent-free. There she began to create the first of what she called her temple dances.

In 1938 she was asked to organize a dance department at Adelphi University. Depending on a small staff of ex-Denishawners, including Jack Cole and Anna Austin, to carry the burden of the teaching, she lectured on religious dance and choreographed several pageants on religious themes. During this same period, with Henrietta Buckmaster as her chosen ghost writer, she completed her autobiography, *An Unfinished Life,* which was published by Harper and Brothers in 1939.

Although no longer greatly in demand as a performer, she did dance in churches and at the New York World's Fair. Curiously, it was Shawn who helped revive her career when in 1941 he invited her to Jacob's Pillow to perform, for the first time in twenty-five years, her famous *Radha, Incense,* and other East Indian solos. For a while thereafter St. Denis shared New York studio-living quarters and school with that other great American lady of ethnic dance, La Meri. Then in 1942, St. Denis moved to California to live with her brother and his family. She dreamed of founding a temple of the dance in Los Angeles, but instead, for practical and patriotic reasons, she contributed to the war effort by working at the Douglas Aircraft factory. When peace came, with help from brother Buzz, she established her Theatre Intime, giving Sunday evening lectures and revivals of her religious dances.

After the war Shawn continued to invite St. Denis to the Pillow as dancer and lecturer. In 1945, he and Miss Ruth gave their first joint concert in fifteen years. The occasion, a benefit for Jacob's Pillow, was held in Carnegie Hall. They performed together at least once annually throughout the next several years.

St. Denis's center remained in Los Angeles, however, where she founded first a Society of Spiritual Arts, then a Church of Divine Dance, and a Rhythmic Choir that performed in several large churches. She often traveled to give lectures, and she received the Capezio Award in 1960 and the Dance Teachers of America award in 1964. At age eighty, she was once asked if she still danced. She replied, with her most enchanting smile, "Well, dear, let's say that I move with remembered beauty." In May, 1966, when she was eighty-seven years old, she made her last public appearance as a dancer, performing at Orange Coast College in California.

During this same period, Shawn had concentrated first on his Men Dancers and then on establishing Jacob's Pillow as an international dance festival. He not only built studios and housing for teachers, staff, pupils, and guest performers, but he continued to develop his own technique and choreography on behalf of his crusade for male dancers. Barton Mumaw, who remained as leading soloist with the Men Dancers through the seven years they toured, has recalled aspects of this era in Shawn's career as teacher and choreographer. What follows is written in the first person as told by Mumaw to the author.

As one of a handful of male pupils at Denishawn House in 1930–1931 I [Barton Mumaw] well remember learning the combination of ballet, Delsarte, Dalcroze, and ethnic movements that Shawn had devised and that came to be known as Denishawn dancing. Although all his life Shawn disliked the term "modern dance" this, for its time, was really what he was teaching. A 1916 prospectus for the Philadelphia Denishawn School described its pupils as dancing "Oriental, classic and modern dance with equal grace." In the 1930s, when an observer remarked about St. Denis's *Cathédrale Engloutie* (to the Debussy music) that, "Her movement is as modern as any I have seen Martha Graham use," Shawn replied with asperity, "Miss Ruth did modern before modern was invented." Shawn himself developed ever more modern technique throughout his teaching career.

When so many of today's dance companies are headed by men like Merce Cunningham, Paul Taylor, Murray Louis, Alvin Ailey, Erik Hawkins, and Arthur Mitchell, it may be difficult to realize that fifty years ago a war had to be fought for the right of American males to participate in serious dance. It may also be easy to forget that the victorious general in this war was Ted Shawn.

The first skirmish took place in 1932. Shawn, now on his own, had lost his equity in Denishawn House and had salvaged only enough money from the sale of his Westport, Connecticut, studio to enable him to purchase a hardscrabble farm in the Berkshires. There he had retired, hoping some day to find the peace, undisturbed by urban demands, that would permit him to develop some fresh creative ideas.

In this difficult period, he had also been restrained from performing until pending litigation could free him from a disastrous contract. Accompanied by a handful of the faithful (pianist Mary Campbell, manager-secretary Margerie Lyon, and a few former Denishawn male dancers) he spent the painful waiting time building and repairing the dilapidated property he was later to develop into the Jacob's Pillow School and Dance Festival. He had little hope of either teaching or dancing in the near future of this Depression era. Then, like a distant bugle resounding over the hills, that May he received an invitation to give a lecture at nearby Springfield College.

Under its official title of International Young Men's Christian Association College, Springfield was the leading school in the United States for physical education teachers, playground directors, and athletic coaches. Undaunted by this rugged reputation, Shawn, with Mary Campbell at the piano, planned to use Jack Cole, Campbell Griggs, Lester Shafer, and me to demonstrate his talk with two of the dances we had done during the last of the Denishawn tours: *Brahms Rhapsody* and *Workers' Songs of Middle Europe*. Since this would be the first time we were to appear before an audience made up entirely of young male athletes, I was filled with trepidation. If Shawn was apprehensive, no one would have guessed it.

As might be expected, we danced in the gymnasium, bare of scenery and nearly as bare of costume. We were astonished by the enthusiastic reception given our dances by the jocks who filled that enormous room. As a result of this single appearance, the head of the College, Dr. L. L. Doggett, asked Shawn to teach a dance semester some time. Ted agreed

Ted Shawn and four of his Men Dancers group in *Brahms Rhapsody*, op. 119, no. 4. Photographed outdoors during rehearsal at Jacob's Pillow, 1932. (Collection Jane Sherman)

on the spot, because this would present an opportunity to spread the gospel of male dancers as artists, and because it would be a chance to make some sorely needed money. Unfortunately, however, Dr. Doggett had to admit that his budget did not permit these classes to be scheduled until a later date. Even though Shawn had no idea how he would manage to live, he offered to teach for no payment if he could begin the first of the year.

A college spokesman announced in the *Springfield Union* of November 10, 1932, that our demonstration had been ". . . 'so revolutionary in quality and so unusual in its work for men that the faculty of the college was deeply interested in Shawn's proposed dance courses.'" The article went on: "It is significant that Springfield is the first college ever to invite a great artist-dancer to join the faculty, and while there has been an increasing amount of interesting material offered to women in this field, there is nothing but folk or tap dancing available for men. It is to fill this need that Mr. Shawn's course is being given."

Back at the Pillow, which we then called the Farm, we began to prepare that course to start in January, 1933. Shawn asked me to be his coteacher and codemonstrator. I had proved I could demonstrate adequately, but teach? When I was only beginning to conquer the problems of my own technique? "Yes!" Ted insisted. "You learn by teaching, you teach by learning. I need you and I know you will do well." We devised exercises, steps, and formations we thought muscle-bound athletes could learn and decided to risk teaching them a group dance that could in no way threaten their image of themselves as he-men. We increased the number of braves in our old *Osage-Pawnee Dance of Greeting* (see pps. 42–43) to include an entire class, hopeful that its primitive rhythms and choreography would be easy to follow.

After celebrating Christmas at Jacob's Pillow, we collected Shawn's teaching materials. We mended and laundered a supply of leotards and dance trunks. Margerie Lyon and Mary Campbell assembled clothes, portable typewriter, and musical scores, like the troupers they were. I packed Ted's bags and my own, stowed everything in the car, locked those Farm doors and windows that had locks, and the four of us were off to Springfield before deep snowfall could trap us on our mountaintop.

With wisdom and foresight, Shawn had insisted that his course be compulsory for every student in the college, so as to obviate the possibility that those men who elected to take it might be called sissies by those who chose not to. Dr. Doggett agreed. He also arranged for Shawn to address the teaching staff and the five hundred members of the student body on the opening day of the semester. Ted, with his customary charm, fluency, and enthusiasm, explained his theory of dance as an ingredient essential to total education, threw in a bit of history of male dancing in other cultures, and stressed the value of dance discipline to the physique of an athlete. His talk was so dignified and so patently sincere that it was greeted with respect rather than with the hostility we had feared.

Nevertheless, we deliberately made our first classes tough. We knew that few of the students had ever seen any real dancing, that some of them resented having to attend (especially when required to wear gym trunks, with their upper torsos and feet bare). We knew others were skeptical, and a handful downright antagonistic. So Shawn, the show-man, had designed initial exercises that he hoped would overcome the reluctance to participate based on ignorance and prejudice. Without music, he and I first demonstrated the vigorous, straightforward movements of running, stretching, leaping, turning, and bending in all directions. Then we asked the men to repeat what we had done as they followed us in a large circle around the slippery gymnasium floor (there were, of course, no barres, no mirrors). We could tell from their puzzled expressions that the movements were proving harder than they had expected, even without the extra effort needed to point toes or straighten knees. We hid our smiles with compassion when footballers began to huff and puff as violently as if they were doing pushups on the practice field.

Subsequently, we sympathized when they limped into class complaining of sore muscles they had never used before. Little by little, we lured each group from exercises into steps, from defiance into cooperation, from sullen obedience into competition with each other. To reach this point, Ted and I created the basic choreography of rowing a boat, using a scythe, chopping down a tree, sawing a plank, sowing grain. As the pupils repeated these "steps" over and over again, we noticed that no one any longer sneered at his classwork as effeminate.

Mary provided American Indian drum music, familiar folk tunes, and Negro spirituals as rhythms most readily identifiable. It was fascinating to watch through the weeks how these sports-conditioned men came to respond unself-consciously to the different moods of the music—came, in short, to dance. Their movements were far from polished, but they were done with a strength and clarity that needed no interpretation. To see a class of young American males of that time move together in these communicative patterns was to glimpse a new development in the ancient art of the dance.

At the end of the course, when each student was required to write an evaluation paper, their reactions were nearly unanimous. Almost every one reported that at first he had believed dancing to be easy, to be unmasculine, and to be a bore, but as the term progressed, he experienced real enjoyment in the release this dance experience gave him, and he hoped that similar courses would be included in all future physical education curricula.

Despite his involvement with teaching, Shawn found the time and energy to rehearse his solos and to perfect my interpretation of *Gnossienne*, one of his most famous dances. He had choreographed this exercise to Satie's music in 1917 as a classroom experiment designed to strengthen body control. When Ruth St. Denis saw him demonstrating it for his pupils one day, she urged him to include the solo in his repertory where it remained for the next thirty years or so, during which time it became an international favorite.

For the stage, Shawn had copied the fresco in the temple at Gnossos in Crete known as *The Cup Bearer,* where the figure wears a strange costume of snakelike rolls of material. As a priest of the Snake Goddess, the dancer performed a ritual that was done with dignity yet contained more than a hint of humor, as if both priest and goddess were amused by a rite that really meant nothing serious to either of them. All movements and formations were kept as much as possible in profile. It was a dance that was brief and difficult and fun to do.

Around the middle of February, just for the challenge of it, we began to coach eight of our most promising Springfield athletes in a theatrical version of the *Osage-Pawnee* dance they had learned in class. Although the beat of the music was easy to follow and the characterization simple, the steps and formations here were more complicated than those we had earlier taught our eight stalwarts. Yet after some weeks of work, Ted and I were confident that when they were properly costumed and lighted, they could appear on stage without bringing shame on our heads. As if in response to our confidence, Shawn was suddenly released from the onerous contract that had prevented his performing. As if in response to that good fortune, he was invited to give nine matinee and evening concerts with a mixed group of girls and boys. These were to be presented at the end of March in Boston, under the unlikely auspices of the Florence Crittendon League for the benefit of its Welcome Home, a refuge established for "the protection and care of delinquent girls."

Ted Shawn in *Gnossienne,* the solo Barton Mumaw performed and had to encore during the first all-male dance concert, Boston, 1933. Photo, Nickolas Muray. (Collection Jane Sherman)

Elated by this opportunity to dance in public again, Shawn accepted the offer before he had the slightest idea of when he would find the time to rehearse, what numbers he could schedule, and even how he could pull a company together. But once more, something had to be done and he did it. He assembled five Denishawn young women to do Denishawn dances they already knew. He called Jack Cole to Springfield to help me break in three talented students for works that required male dancers. We got the necessary old costumes down from the Farm and the necessary new ones made.

We decided to add our eight Springfield "Indians" to the last dance of our group of Negro spirituals. This meant we had to instruct them how to "distress" the costumes they were to wear. Work pants and cotton work shirts had been bought for them to size, and were therefore bright and new. To give them the worn look Shawn demanded, he showed each man how to drag the pants through mud, let them dry, then drag them and dry them again and again until they appeared thoroughly beat up. Then, despite some grumbles, he insisted that they rip the hems of their sleeves into ragged edges, and dip the shirts in a strong solution of tea to give them the correct work-stained shade. And he made them continue the process until he was completely satisfied with the results.

Against all odds, we were finally ready for our opening concert on March 20, but not before we had lived through some hilarious moments. One Sunday, for example, we were rehearsing in the Springfield studio of Anatole Bourmann (the ballet teacher and author of a biography of Nijinsky). Everyone froze in mid-leap at the sound of sudden loud knocking and the shouted command, "Open up! Police!" Sure that an escaped thief or murderer must be hiding on the premises, I ran to open the door on a pair of stern-faced cops, one of whom announced that we were all under arrest.

"What for?" Shawn demanded as he hastened to place himself between his startled brood and this unexpected menace. "For dancing on the Sabbath, *that's* what for," he was told in no uncertain tones. "And *that's* breaking the Blue Laws of the Commonwealth."

Ted protested fiercely that we were only perfecting our "art," an argument that fell on deaf ears. He then exerted his considerable powers of persuasion to plead ignorance and innocence and to promise to "reform." At that, the officers agreed to let us off with a warning if we stopped the rehearsal at once. We needed no further word of encouragement to scurry to the dressing-rooms and get into our street clothes. We heaved a collective sigh of relief when we reassembled, thankful that we had been spared the humiliation of being hauled away in the paddy-wagon in our bathing suits. Locking the studio door behind us, Ted walked down the street with me. He was outraged and furious, and he kept muttering imprecations against Bourmann who, he firmly believed, had set the police on us—a suspicion that was not as paranoid as it might now seem, because back in those days proponents of ballet had been known physically to assault proponents of modern dance in theatre lobbies.

Then came the comical hour when our eight athletes were introduced to their costumes for the *Osage-Pawnee* dance. Since I had been left in charge of these details, it was up to me to get each of my redskins into a chamois-cloth cap Ted and I had made to imitate a shaved skull, each cap sprouting a topknot of feathers. There was a lot of horseplay and war whoops in the lockerroom when the men first looked at themselves in the mirror. It took some time before I could calm them down sufficiently to dress each one in an outfit that consisted only of two panels of decorated buckskin hanging fore and aft over a minimal G-string, leaving their bottoms, for all practical purposes, uncovered. My warriors reacted with collective shock when it dawned on them that, in the course of their dance, the exposure would be considerable.

Having performed this dance myself, I understood their apprehension and hastened to assure them that everything would be most respectable because the orange red lighting would be dim, and their bodies would be entirely covered with a deep red-tan paint. The howls of rage that greeted this piece of news would have made an enemy Iroquois shiver with terror. Before I completely lost my courage, I blurted out that they would also have to shave.

"You mean we have to shave *there*, for Christ's sake?" one of the more hirsute young Hercules yelled.

I swallowed an impulse to chide him for using profanity on Christian territory as I explained in a shaky voice that Massachusetts law did not permit the showing of pubic hair in public. From the expression on their faces, I was no longer convinced we would have eight Indians to perform our opening number.

Came the day of the first concert at the Boston Repertory Theatre, a conventional Denishawn program featuring the five girls and the five men of the regular company. Came, too, the day of double disaster: President Roosevelt closed the banks and Ted Shawn dislocated his sacroiliac.

Because of this unexpected Depression-induced bank holiday, the average man and woman was left with no more than the cash in his hand—hardly money that any sane person would dare spend on theatre tickets. Because of his injury, it was feared that Shawn could not dance, yet he was bound and determined that our show must go on. He announced that scrip would be accepted at the box-office in lieu of coin of the realm. (This decision put him no more than ten dollars in the red at the end of the engagement, a Pyrrhic victory if ever there was one.) He also informed his physician that he would dance.

Faced with granite stubbornness, the doctor reluctantly strapped his patient into a corset of wide, heavy adhesive tape that was hidden beneath Shawn's briefest costume. Although it was supportive when first applied, this brace weakened under the strain and sweat of dancing. It therefore became my dreaded duty after every performance to rip off the old tape so that the new could be put on. Ted's screams during this operation might well have been heard as far away as the Old North Church. By the end of the week, that whole area of his body was a mass of torn skin and blisters.

But our program of Tuesday, March 21, 1933, made up for both pain and panic. Purely as an experiment, Shawn had scheduled for that single night serious dances done only by males, the first such American modern concert. Since I was to perform *Gnossienne* in this unique venture, I was unforgettably nervous. Yet I must have danced well, judging by the cloudburst of applause after I exited. Ted was standing in the wings. He told me to take another bow, then still another. Finally, he signaled Mary at the piano onstage, gave me a push on the bare shoulder, and, with a big grin, whispered, "Give it to them again, Barton! Give it to them again!" So I did, and that, too, was unforgettable.

I no longer remember how we got our recalcitrant braves shaved, painted, made up, costumed, and on stage for their history-making debut, but they were astonishingly effective in their opening number. Furthermore, considering that they had never had a chance to rehearse with the full company, they were very good in *Calvary*, which concluded the program. In this, the ensemble of thirteen men, led by Shawn, was somberly lighted from opposite wings of the stage, their shadows adding dark patterns to the slow, marchlike formations of the work. As a critic from the *Montreal Star* was later to write, "The religious dances which brought the program to a close were in some respects the best of all. . . . All the Negro Spirituals were danced perfectly, alike as to rhythm and to emotional values." We felt it was a real triumph that our eight amateurs could project the intensity of those of us who were professionals.

The audience reaction at the close of the concert was memorable. There had never been anything to equal such applause in our experience after concerts that had included girl dancers. Ted, Jack, and I were stunned. Our Springfield recruits grinned as if they didn't know what had hit them, as they took the countless bows with us, shuffling from one bare foot to another. When at last the houselights were brought up to disperse the audience, we left the stage together like a football team that had just scored the winning touchdown.

In his dressing-room, after the well-wishers had greeted him, been greeted by him, and departed, Ted stood in a daze. He did not so much as wince when I ripped the adhesive from his raw flesh. We were both close to tears that had nothing to do with physical suffering. Then, matter-of-factly, he put on his robe, sat down at his dressing-table, and began to remove his makeup. He paused, towel in hand, just long enough to look up at my reflection in the mirror and say, softly, "This means the time has come. The time has really come."

That was the moment Shawn and His Men Dancers was born.

In his 1940 book *Dance We Must,* Shawn expressed his fundamentals of dance education as follows:

A dancer must have mastered all those fundamental movement patterns of swinging, running, walking, leaping, jumping, falling, torsion, bending, shaking, oppositions, successions, parallelisms; in short, the "alphabet" of those movements out of which dance steps are made. He must be the master of the twin principles of tension and relaxation. He must be able to maintain balance perfectly whether at rest or in motion. He must have his body so trained and so coordinated that the idea, be it kinetic, musical or dramatic, is expressed by his whole body as a unit. He must know thoroughly all the patterns of construction of dance in relation to all three dimensions of space, and in relation to that fourth dimension of the dance, time. He must be trained in the relation of the dance to music, so that his movement and the music seem the twin emanations of one impulse, and he must master the relationship of himself to a group of other dancers in an almost infinite variety of patterns.

The exercises, the dances that Shawn used as his teaching tools did not arise coldly in the brain to find expression solely through the muscles. When I witnessed the stupendous effort he expended in class and rehearsals during the early days at Jacob's Pillow, I once asked him, "Is it worth all you have to do to step out in that stage?" His answer was instantaneous and vehement. "It is worth it! You see, Barton, dancing is like making love, and how often do we experience *that* kind of perfect fulfillment? But when it does happen, there is no sensation to compare with it, unless perhaps what a saint experiences at the instant of illumination. That is what keeps us slaving, the hope for that instant of illumination in a rare perfect performance." Which would he choose, I wondered aloud: "a perfect love act or a heavenly dance moment?" "The dance! The dance! Always the dance! Because it alone can strengthen those qualities that will sustain a dancer through all the other experiences of his life."

He badly needed that sustenance at the Pillow when the first all-male group was formed because he had to mastermind every detail. I was his "sorcerer's apprentice" who sometimes felt he was drowning under more responsibilities than he should have assumed. Shawn often saved us from despair, and he eventually disciplined us into a respectable working unit with his daily routine. He believed, as Dr. Jonathan Miller nearly half a century later was to write in his book *The Body in Question*, "The body is the medium of experience and the instrument of action." This is a simple observation until one tries to incorporate experience and action in dance, but Shawn aimed to achieve this physical incorporation through the following schedule, to which his Men Dancers adhered as faithfully as possible:

7–8 A.M. Breakfast.

8–10 A.M. Studio. Warming-up exercises, on floor and upright, to stretch and strengthen muscles and acquire fluidity. These varied as Shawn invented new ones. Then fundamental barre to develop technique, dexterity, and body line. Next, open floor for single steps, then a combination of those steps into dance phrases (enchainements, in ballet terms). We moved to piano music, to recited poetry, to singing, chanting, percussion, and/or no sound at all. Class ended with a repetition of sections of work in progress.

10–Noon Rehearsal of group by Shawn of current repertory.

Noon–2 P.M. Gathering on platform outside studio (if the sun shone). Lunch in the nude, followed by Shawn's reading aloud to us. (Some of this was heavy going—Gilbert Murray on Greek poetry, Ouspensky's *Tertium Organum,* Havelock Ellis, Aristophanes, Goethe. But Ted also read news from the morning paper, selections from *archie and mehitabel,* a Robert Benchley humorous essay, and even quips from Groucho Marx on the theory, I suppose, that all thought and no laughter make a dull dancer.)

2–3 P.M.   Studio. Review of repertory and work on new compositions, under my supervision.

3–5 P.M.   Outside chores to maintain and improve the property.

5–6 P.M.   Shower, rest, and social hour (for those not assigned to prepare dinner).

6–7 P.M.   Dinner.

7–Bed   Work on costumes, props, addressing and folding circulars, preparation of press material, or whatever other sitting-down chores had to be done.

It was a constant battle to stick to this routine despite aches, pains, blisters, injuries, minor illnesses, and the urgent menial tasks that often demanded immediate attention. We tried, however. Many a night I left the others to their chores before the fireplace to go to the studio alone and work on my own choreography or polish a new solo Shawn had created for me. As dancers will, I repeated one phrase many, many times. (Later, when working with fellow ex-Denishawner Jack Cole in Hollywood, I remember his struggling with a single eight-bar passage for an entire day.) Once when I was practicing very late in the studio, a guest in the Pillow farmhouse heard a brief section of my music played over and over on the gramophone as I labored with rhythm and line. The next morning, instead of complaining at having been kept awake, he praised my industry and left a check for $75 with Ted as a present for me!

The Men Dancers became effective performers because Shawn had the gift of being able to create and teach movement that was original yet immediately understood by an audience. It cannot be repeated too often that the public of the 1930s was deeply prejudiced against serious male dancers. Our acceptance would confirm Shawn's intuition that to overcome prejudice, men's dancing should be based on familiarity with male physical limitations and abilities, as well as on recognition of the work and ideals that were at the time considered masculine. He even went so far as to claim that strong, harsh, broad movements corresponded to the lower, or masculine, section of the musical gamut, whereas the softer, more typical feminine movements corresponded to the gamut above middle C. He later conceded that there was a discrepancy in this arbitrary differentiation, but he never entirely abandoned his belief.

One of the bits of technique he taught us that beautifully combined the masculine and the feminine were the held-breath *luft* pauses that have come to be known in modern dance as suspensions. From him, I learned that a dance suspension resembles a singer's voice descending from a high to a low note in a single, delicate, smooth phrase. There comes a moment of balance when the movement is clearly etched in space like a breaking wave before it overflows and falls into a resolution. Nijinsky is said to have had this quality of floating at the apogee of a leap. The emphasis on such quality of movement characterized Pillow training, in contrast with many of today's techniques where dance titles may change but movement quality remains the same.

Shawn encouraged us to create our own dances, and he included several works choreographed by his Men Dancers in their regular programs (nineteen during the seven years, of which six were mine). It was not until we worked together in the early days at Jacob's Pillow, however, that I had had the opportunity to observe Ted as a choreographer. It was a revelation in action of the philosophy he had expressed in one of the lectures he had given at George Peabody College in Tennessee: He said,

The dance must have sequence, each movement done must lead inevitably into the next movement, so that one could not imagine any other movement being possible as successor to the movement just done. This implies architecture absolutely. The whole dance, as a work of art, must be constructed as well and carefully as a beautiful building, which is beautiful not only because of its materials and ornamentation, but also on account of its design, its proportions: because it has a solid foundation, and because its walls are solid and capable of supporting the roof. A dance work of art must have a beginning, development, and climax just as a building has foundations, walls and roof.

Somehow, in the midst of the stress of building the Farm into a habitable dwelling-place and studio, Shawn had found the time and energy to plan the music, movements, costumes, and lighting for ten new numbers for an upcoming tour. From the first company get-together to final dress rehearsal, the man knew exactly what he wanted each of us to do. But when I alone was permitted to watch him develop his great solo *O Brother Sun and Sister Moon,* I was amazed to see how

he struggled through trial and error to reveal in dance the message and
the emotion he sought to express. He explained to me that for nearly a
decade before he began to create this work he had studied the life of St.
Francis of Assisi in writings, paintings, statues, and woodcuts. His
accumulated contemplation inspired each step he set to Respighi's
music. His integrity was as patent as his effort and he kept this solo in
his repertory to the end of his performing days.

When Shawn and I discussed his specific choreography I quickly
discovered that it was wise to present my reactions in such a way that, if
my ideas should be incorporated into the dance, they appeared to be his
own. Whenever I asked him for advice on my own choreographic
attempts he responded with such impersonal, helpful interest that I
experienced none of the nervousness an apprentice feels in showing his
works to a master. And in evaluating the creations of other dancers,
Shawn never insisted that they must do anything his way. His sole
concern was to shape the material into viable form, by trimming or
enlarging it into an effective whole.

To fulfill his aim of shaping his all-male group into professionals,
Shawn led us through hours in which each one learned not only his own
faults and talents but those of the ensemble as a unit. These were the
hours when we came to know Shawn, the choreographer, to the fullest.
More meticulous, demanding, and inspiring even than Shawn the
teacher, the choreographer used us as raw material that embodied his
visions. But heaven help the man who proved recalcitrant or sluggish.
He became the immediate target of a memorable hot-tempered tongue-
lashing. Yet this was forgotten by Ted as soon as we left the studio,
because there was nothing personal in his rages. He was clear, concise,
and efficient in rehearsals, and we valued the bare bones of the art
experience that he gave us. Lacking as it did any of the glamor of
performing in a theatre, this experience came straight out of our lives
and our labor together, something that only a very fortunate few can
ever enjoy.

As we learned new roles and perfected old ones, we sensed that
Shawn had created a style of movement that audiences would respect.
Powerful as it was expressive, it gave us the confidence to venture out
into a hostile world. He also created within us a feeling for the ensemble
that those who later tried to restage his works found impossible to
duplicate. When the Men Dancers performed together, no one of us
tried to outshine the others and thereby destroy their performance as
well as his own. We may have been competitive in our efforts to

improve, but we were never allowed to be competitive on stage. Such discipline, imposed on us by Shawn, produced unusual group work that contemporary critics were quick to recognize and praise.

This may be the logical place to insert a word about writers who were too young to have seen Shawn on stage and who certainly were never privileged to have watched him during his creative labors. One wonders where they get the authority, not to say the audacity, to question Shawn's abilities. Here is a man who taught for fifty-five years and from whose classes developed five of this country's most influential dance figures. A man whose works were cheered in the United States, Canada, Cuba, Germany, Switzerland, England, and every important nation in the Far East. Who, between 1914 and 1931, created one hundred eighty-five dances and nine major ballets for Denishawn, co-creating with Ruth St. Denis another three ballets. And who, from 1933 to 1940, choreographed for his Men Dancers fifty-seven group or solo dances and six large-scale ballets, two of which earned the distinction of being the first full-evening productions of contemporary dance works. As Shawn was to write in his *One Thousand and One Night Stands,* "The next such work was not premiered until twenty years later when Martha Graham presented her *Clytemnestra* at the Adelphi Theatre in New York."

Shawn's first full-length work, *O, Libertad!,* premiered on October 7, 1936, in Garden City, New York. It was presented in three sections. Act I, entitled "The Past," concentrated on the history of early California from the "Noche Triste de Moctezuma," for Shawn and the entire company, through solos and ensemble numbers of the "Penitentes," "Peonage," the "Hacendado," and the "Forty-niners." Act II, entitled "The Present," opened with "Olympiad," in which the Men Dancers represented various sport activities in dance, and continued with aspects of war, the "Jazz Decade," modernism, and a "March of the Veterans of Future Wars." Act III, under the title of "Kinetic Molpai," consisted of a series of abstract dances that mounted in originality of movement to a high level of excitement.

Dance of the Ages, the second of Shawn's full-evening works, premiered on October 7, 1938, in Amherst, Massachusetts. This was programmed in four acts that covered all aspects of movement quality from tribal culture based on the element Fire, to city-state-philosophic culture based on the element Water, to democratic-political culture based on the element Earth, to the aspirations of the future and the culture of the creative artist based on the element Air. The music for

Basketball, from Olympiad Suite in *O, Libertad*! Barton Mumaw at far right.
Photographed in rehearsal at Jacob's Pillow, 1937, by John Lindquist. (Collection Jane Sherman)

both these outstanding productions, *O, Libertad!* and *Dance of the Ages,* was especially composed by Jess Meeker.

As he himself would be the first to admit, not all Shawn's creations were masterpieces, nor did his every appearance merit an ovation. Yet in his day, acclaim for his choreography and performance were equally unanimous and practically universal, from the American reviewer who wrote in 1922 that "[*Invocation to the*] *Thunderbird* was superbly done by Mr. Shawn in a costume which was as correctly magnificent as it was brief, and which set off his perfect figure to the greatest advantage"; to the Tokyo *Macho-Shinbun* critic of 1925 who reported, "We say at once that Mr. Shawn is the finest male dancer we have ever seen. . . . The great art of Denishawn should not be missed by anyone in Japan"; to the reviews of the Men Dancers when Walter Terry in the *Boston Herald* of March 12, 1938, wrote that "*O Libertad!* is in most respects the greatest dance creation that America has yet produced." Following our Carnegie Hall concert, a critic for the *Brooklyn Citizen* of February 21, 1940, wrote, "Mr. Shawn is unquestionably the greatest living male dancer." Terry, reporting for the *New York Herald Tribune* of that same date, claimed that "*Kinetic Molpai* is one of the finest group compositions that the dance has ever produced." I find it difficult to understand how it is possible for today's writers accurately to assess the value of this artist within the context of his era unless, like contemporary critics, they had seen the bulk of Shawn's choreography and experienced the impact of his dancing in person.

Shawn in his prime was not only a technically skilled and exciting dancer, he was a master programmer. I was always so busy backstage that I rarely had the chance to see him perform. But one season I did watch his solo concert from out front. I saw with what cunning he built up the audience response dance by dance, relentlessly, until, almost as at a religious revival, he had them on their feet, shouting, at the end. Adulation did not make him smug, however. As Miss Ruth once wrote of him, "He was a rare, forceful person, capable of great singleness of purpose and an artist of fine concepts, carried into execution with skill and style, while underneath he was always growing spiritually, desiring passionately to find his real selfhood." Doyen critic John Martin, even though his heart was basically with the ex-Denishawn pioneer rebels, described Shawn in his book, *America Dancing,* as "Keen of wit, caustic of tongue, avid of interest, terrifically temperamental, of inexhaustible energy, tenacious, aggressive, indomitable. Obviously of the stuff to break down barriers and become the first male dancer in America to achieve a position of influence and importance."

The Men Dancers in *Kinetic Molpai*. Barton Mumaw second from left. Photo, Shapiro. (Collection Barton Mumaw)

Only years later, when the derogatory term "macho" came into wide usage, did writers so describe those works for his Men Dancers with which Shawn "broke down barriers." They forgot, if they had ever known of them, his first all-male ensemble work, the *Pyrrhic Dance* created for sixteen warriors as part of the Dance Pageant of India, Greece, and Egypt that he and St. Denis presented at the University of California Greek Theatre in Berkeley as far back as 1916, and his intensely virile Denishawn solos throughout the 20s. They forgot, if they ever knew it, that only by being what is now called macho could Shawn and his company have been accepted by the American public in that era when many barriers remained to be broken.

Yet despite the emphasis on masculinity there were elements in Shawn's choreography that dared a tenderness far in advance of the mores of his society. This was demonstrated in the first solo he created for me, in 1931, *Pierrot in the Dead City,* to music from Erich Korngold's opera *Die Tote Stadt.* Of this work, which Shawn did not consider me mature enough to perform in public until 1935, Lucien Price, the distinguished author and critic for the *Boston Globe,* wrote in a 1937 letter to Shawn: "It is anybody's lost youth including, alas! some day, Barton's own. . . . The beauty, the wistfulness, the yearning, the gaiety and tenderness, the grace and the fleeting joy that are packed into those brief moments of the dance are great lyric poetry and I don't wonder that it can make people weep. It is the pathos of human life that it is so beautiful, and so brief. Which is exactly what the dance itself is."

I learned from Shawn, teacher and choreographer, that in youth, simply from the sheer gifts of litheness and agility, one gets credit for more than is really there. Next comes the hard, discriminating labor when the machine must be trained physically, mentally, and emotionally. Then at last, if you are lucky, you acquire the technique, the confidence, and the courage to dare to dance as you wish. This is what produces those few moments in a dancer's career when everything goes superbly. The audience is receptive, the music is in perfect accord with you, the lighting cues are precise, the costume seems part of your body, you don't drop any props, you don't fall flat on your face on a slippery stage, and you move through space like an angel. Such moments can be counted on the fingers of one-and-a-half hands over a lifetime. But they are what keeps a dancer going. They were what kept Shawn going for sixty of his eighty years despite the bittersweet knowledge that the Celestial Pub-Keeper could at any moment announce, "Time, please, gentlemen."

Now, some years after that announcement ended Shawn's life, I believe he is beginning to be recognized for his true worth, as Lucien Price evaluated it in the *Boston Sunday Globe* of August 19, 1962:

To have done something of such artistic significance that the cultural history of a nation is altered is surely the work of a great man. To have done that three times is the work of a genius . . . three times Shawn has made a major contribution to the United States and world culture . . . his work as a dancer, his fight for the role of the male dancer, and his founding of the unique university of the dance [at Jacob's Pillow] are accomplishments unmatched in the artistic history of this country.

Postscript

In *The Beleaguered City* (1949) Ruth St. Denis wrote:

I am asking for a new freedom for the artists of America, freedom from the prison walls of our comfort-loving life, our incessant commercialism and our abject adoration of fashions. . . . I want freedom from the current trends of obscure, involved, conscious intellectualisms and unconscious insanities into the pure free air of noble inspiration and clear visions of beauty.

When she formed the Ruth St. Denis Center in California in 1962, she wrote what might be considered an addendum to her dream:

I believe in the Ministry of Beauty. I believe in the Divinity of the Arts. I believe that Art is the Ark of the Covenant in which all ideals of beauty and excellence are carried before the race. It is a pillar of cloud by day and of fire by night. I hereby offer my services and my God-given talents to the avowed purpose of this Center and pledge my allegiance to the ideals of Ruth St. Denis.

As St. Denis may have considered this her crowning achievement, Shawn considered Jacob's Pillow his, despite the inconceivable difficulties, the constant financial worries, and the unceasing demands it made on his stamina. He hinted at the cost he had paid for this achievement in 1957 at the Silver Jubilee celebration of the Pillow's founding. For this occasion, he had danced the role of King Lear in *Sundered Majesty,* choreographed by Myra Kinch. In his curtain speech he announced sadly but with humor, "Running Jacob's Pillow for twenty-five years has given me all the experience necessary to portray madness convincingly!"

The last thing Shawn published before his death was a four-page pamphlet entitled *Credo,* from which the following are quotations:

I believe that dance is the oldest, noblest, and most cogent of the arts.

I believe that dance is the most perfect symbol of the activity of God and His angels.

I believe that dance has the power to heal, mentally and physically.

I believe that true education in the art of dance is education of the whole man—his physical, mental and emotional natures are disciplined and nourished simultaneously in dance.

I believe that dance is the universal language, and as such has the power to promote One World. Dance can replace misunderstandings due to verbalization which distorts communications between the nations and races of mankind.

I believe that dance communicates man's deepest, highest and most truly spiritual thoughts and emotions far better than words, written or spoken.

I believe that DANCE is a way of life, which will lead humanity into continually higher and greater dimensions of existence.

From their statements of belief, it can be seen that through the long years of public and private differences, through divergences of paths and ambitions, Ruth St. Denis and Ted Shawn did indeed maintain a Denishawn unity.

That unity was celebrated onstage for the last time at their golden wedding anniversary in 1964. At Jacob's Pillow they performed *Siddhas of the Upper Air,* a duet they had especially created for this event. It was based on a St. Denis poem of the same title, which had been inspired by an East Indian miniature. The music was composed by Jess Meeker.

In the blue spaces between the stars,
The siddhas stand together,
Blown by the lifting winds of the whirling worlds
They move side by side with the effortless motion of
A divine dance.

Gazing ahead, their hearts beat to the
Unearthly rhythm of perfected love.

They are going towards the light of an unimaginable sun!
Their garments are blown behind them
Like a comet's saffron tail.

Shawn wrote Barton Mumaw details of "the onslaught of press, radio, and TV . . . the crew coming on from Hollywood to film the new duet Ruth and I premiered for a documentary on Ruth's life, which is soon to be shown," and then described the dance. St. Denis wore a saffron sari, he a saffron dhoti and turban. With a minimum of movement but in their usual floating style, they drifted through subtle lighting to a climax of the two-as-one. With Shawn slightly in the lead, advancing in a slow, dramatic walk in profile, they disappeared together up an inclined ramp into the wings, their heads high, their eyes fixed on the "light of an unimaginable sun."

When Shawn some time later spoke the commentary for a film entitled *Fifty Years of Dance,* he concluded his description of this final Denishawn duet as "The two of us were going up and up and up, remembering all the love of the earth but still lovers of infinite distance and infinite space, and still always up, going up."

Ruth St. Denis died of a heart attack in 1968 at age eighty-nine. The words of another of her poems are engraved on her vault at Forest Lawn Cemetery in California:

The Gods have meant
That I should dance
And in some mystic hour
I shall move to unheard rhythms
Of the cosmic orchestra of heaven
And you will know the language
Of my wordless poems
And will come to me
For that is why I dance.

Ted Shawn died of a heart attack in 1972 at age eighty. His ashes are buried at the rock that is Jacob's Pillow. A plaque affixed to it reads:

Ted Shawn
1891 – 1972

Founder of
Jacob's Pillow
Dance Festival

R.I.P., our parents.

Chapter Nine
Thoughts On Reviving Denishawn

I AM CONVINCED THERE is a special problem in re-creating Denishawn works, even the ones for which choreographic notes survive. It is a problem that those who revive a classic ballet do not share. With classic ballets, the theatrical continuity of story, setting, music, style, costume, and choreography has been maintained for generations as handed down from the original performers to their descendents through long-established companies, and the vocabulary of the steps is a universal esperanto.

True, Baryshnikov may stage his own version of the venerable *Nutcracker,* but he works from well-documented tradition. True, *Giselle's* steps may improve with modern technical disciplines and stronger, better-designed toe shoes, but her truth persists in spite of recent critical questions as to whether we are now seeing the honest-to-goodness, one hundred per cent pure, original choreography in these old ballets.

Reconstructors who wish to keep alive the works of Humphrey, Weidman, Graham, Tamiris, Holm, Limón, and other early modern dance innovators may have the essential help not only of notes and films but, far more important, of dancers who performed in those works. Many of Ted Shawn's late 1930s dances have been preserved for present-day audiences by Barton Mumaw, either through his own performances or through his coaching of the Alvin Ailey Company, Norman Walker, Clive Thompson, Richard Cragun, and others. Thus the bodies of classic ballet and modern dance exist to be revitalized with conscientious care. But with Denishawn, a corpse must be disinterred for resuscitation.

Why is this? Because, after Ruth St. Denis and Ted Shawn separated following the 1931 Lewisohn Stadium concert, there was a 40-year break in continuity between the last real Denishawn Company and concert and the reconstruction in the 1970s of some Denishawn works by former teachers or students. I attribute the distortions I found in those reconstructions to this break in continuity. For in order to breathe life into a Denishawn work it is not enough to have revived it from paper or film or learned it second-hand in a studio. Ideally, the revivalist needs to have absorbed through professional osmosis the magic that St. Denis and Shawn instilled into even their minor creations. Otherwise Denishawn revivals can mislead dance historians who have no other means of determining the quality and the actual appearance of the original works.

In the reconstructions I have seen, and in my own recent experiences as a reconstructor, the spirit of Denishawn Americana and ethnic works survives its transition from another age better than the abstract music visualizations. It may be that today's dancers find it impossible to empathize with these impersonal dances of the past, which they may misunderstand as being spineless because they seem simplistic in form, content, and choice of music. It may be they find it easier to duplicate the intricacy and forcefulness of ethnic and folk works, or it may be that it is always less difficult to perform in character and in costume than as one's undisguised self.

It goes without saying that no contemporary performer can project the presence of a St. Denis, a Shawn, a Humphrey, or a Weidman. Nor have audiences the right to expect that this can be done. Those of us who worked with them, however, especially feel the lack of their conviction in the revivals of their dances. For it must be emphasized that "presence" was also evident in the emotional intensity with which the least of the Denishawn Dancers performed their ensemble parts.

Our bodies were stockier and weightier than the Balanchine ideal, and we were not as finely-tuned technical instruments. But a quality of integrity pervaded our work that today's dancers find difficult to recapture when they attempt Denishawn re-creations. Murray Louis, writing on revivals in his splendid book *Inside Dance*, expresses the problem perfectly: "An overly trained dancer does not have the skill to bring richness to simplicity." And therein lies the rub.

Is it possible to re-create Denishawn works in such a way as to duplicate their original impact? This key question has been made, will continue to be made, and should be made, because St. Denis and Shawn were the products of their era in dance. They were rebels and in-novators, prophets and pioneers with unshakable belief in their message, as well as being hard-nosed professionals forced to earn a living for themselves, their company and their school. Perhaps it is inevitable that those who lack a similar background can at best only mirror the image without revealing its depths.

Here are some examples of what I mean: in the issue of *Smithsonian* for October, 1980, two of many photographs illustrate an article devoted to a program of dance revivals. One shows St. Denis in her early famous solo *Incense*. She is poised in a plain sari and choli, her downcast eyes fixed on a simple tray that holds the incense from which faint smoke is rising. It is a dimly lit moment of reverent mysticism. On the opposite page, the dancer who is re-creating this work is pictured posed in a brilliant spotlight. She wears a red bodice and ʌivid blue sari, with an elaborately jewelled breastplate and headdress. She beams a wide, vacant smile as she gazes up to her left hand arched over her head, completely ignoring the ornate silver dish of burning incense she holds in her right. No more than a single glance at these two photographs is needed to convince the viewer how deeply St. Denis was involved in a religious ritual, and how little the younger dancer understood the meaning of the dance.

As part of a program presented at Jacob's Pillow, a performer presented her version of St. Denis's *Dance of the Red and Gold Sari*. In this, to quote Deborah Jowitt in the *Village Voice* (August 31, 1982), she was "seductively robing and disrobing herself for a lover . . . [with] the dark, hot stares of an exotic stripper." Poor Miss Ruth! As anyone who had ever seen her in this dance would know, she intended merely to enact a chatty, respectable, and respected salesperson who was demonstrating the beauties of a sari to a prospective buyer. During her charming and innocent sales pitch, she demonstrated to the audience the proper way an East Indian woman puts on the 6-yard-long by 39-inches-wide material that is her dress.

To my mind, these glaring misrepresentations are unforgivable. No matter how exact or inexact the choreography, such severe violations of the original intentions of spirit, costume, and lighting are cruelty not only to the memory of great artists but to present-day dance researchers who seek and long to perpetuate validity.

Let me describe how some Denishawn ensemble music visualizations have been reconstructed. When I saw a 1976 revival of Miss Ruth's *Second Arabesque* (see pps. 51–52) the young dancers wore short, full-skirted so-called Grecian tunics of blue nylon. Their hair fell to their waists, unbound. In relentless blue-white lighting, they moved with

Ruth St. Denis at Jacob's Pillow, 1948, where she danced *The Dance of the Red and Gold Sari* in this adaptation of the original costume. Photo, John Lindquist. (Collection Jane Sherman)

coltish exuberance in off-the-ground skips and leaps, long hair flying, short skirts flaring, in what seemed perilously like a burlesque of "interpretive" dancing. Gone were the ankle-length, faintly golden-colored chiffon costumes St. Denis had copied from her studies of Tanagra figurines. Gone the wigs of high-piled controlled curls. Gone the rose-tawny lighting that suggested a Tanagra vase. Gone the tiptoe-ing dancers tall and elegant as three lighted candles.

Walter Terry might have been criticizing this kind of distortion in a sadly apt metaphor he once used: "... [it] could be compared with a reconstructed Indian village in which the tepees were made of plastic and secured with aluminum poles instead of being built with the hides and boughs of real life." (*Smithsonian,* October, 1980). He might have been referring to the lovely St. Denis-Humphrey *Soaring.* As has been noted the five dancers wore Dutch-cut, blonde wigs and silk fleshings, and appeared to be nude when we performed with the large, square, grey-green silk veil that was the focus—indeed, the sixth dancer—of the group. Yet despite the evidence of photographs taken during the Deni-shawn life of this dance, current companies persist in garbing their dancers in fluttering skirts, and in permitting their individual long, varicolored tresses to fly free, thus destroying the impersonality of the work by shifting emphasis from the veil to each of the dancers. I suspect such unprofessional modesty reflects a dancing-school mentality that ignores, or is ignorant of, theatrical elements.

The monotonous blue-green lighting favored by most revivalists vitiates another essential ingredient in this most frequently recon-structed of all Denishawn works. The lighting Miss Ruth had devised for her *Soaring,* with psychedelic effects far in advance of their day, changed with the moods of the music and the choreography from green sea to pale blue sky, to dark blue-green-rolling waves, to rose and violet flower figures, to red and orange flames. Only lately have attempts been made to duplicate these original effects.

(It may be of interest historically to note that co-creator Doris Hum-phrey, Martha Graham, Louise Brooks, and many other Denishawn Dancers, including the author, performed in *Soaring.* Even Shawn as well as Charles Weidman, danced the center role briefly during a tour of England in 1922, because there were only four female dancers in that company. Doris, on hearing of this, said she found it thoroughly unsuit-able to introduce a male figure into such an ephemeral dance. By similar force of circumstance, similar changes were frequently made in Deni-shawn repertory works.)

Many of the other reconstructed Denishawn group dances I have observed are those in which I had either appeared or had seen performed countless times when I was a member of the company. I am not ashamed to confess that watching them, my tears of nostalgia have often turned to tears of rage. But anger does not generate clarity. If I view the problem calmly, I know I do not have the answer as how best Denishawn works can be kept alive and accurate. Nor, in criticizing their efforts, do I belittle those who have tried to do this, for I have learned from experience how difficult it is.

For example, when I started to reconstruct three rather simple music visualizations that had been choreographed to Chopin music and that I knew well, I quickly discovered that my young performers' bodies, training, and feeling for music were vastly different from mine. They could translate the steps from my notes and word descriptions, but when I spoke to them of an unending, flowing quality of movement, of breathing with the music, of merging their minds and muscles with the fabric they were manipulating, I spoke a foreign language. As Tobi Tobias wrote about the dancers in the latest resurrection of *Soaring* (*New York,* April 26, 1982): "They suffered from overly taut legs and feeble arms." And, I might add in my experience with some young dancers, from a coldly rigid solar plexus and insensitivity to the music.

All the correct lighting, costuming, choreography, and good will in the world cannot disguise these basic flaws. For how does a reconstructor ask a good dancer *not* to be a good dancer? How does one tactfully tell her that she really need not count a waltz? How does one impart the convictions of an older generation to a younger? I failed to find definitive answers to these questions and had to be content with preserving the spirit of Miss Ruth's dances as authentically as we did.

Perhaps it is impossible for the intensities of the artists of a certain period to be visited on those of a later one. Perhaps this is a basic reason why Denishawn re-creations are often unsatisfying to "one who was there." And perhaps, this is why I sensed that the movements were almost always too slow, too bland, too ladylike. Because of this pervading adagio enervation, I sometimes had to restrain myself from crying out during the performance of a well-loved number, "Faster! Faster! Stronger! Leap higher!" For I well knew that even in the most elfin of Miss Ruth's music visualizations or the frothiest of Papa's waltzes, a determined muscular, emotional purpose informed the grace and fluidity of every step.

Before I wrote the above words, I questioned myself strictly to see if I were attributing to these dances qualities they did not in reality possess. In so doing, I think I passed the litmus test that proves those qualities did exist: while a dancer may forget specific choreography, no one can doubt the autonomic veracity of kinesthetic memory. This is acquired through years of doing the same dances over and over again on stage until their dynamics, their tempi, their extensions, their vigor, all become part of one's nerves and bones. It is also acquired, by the sort of osmosis I have indicated, from long and intimate performing contact with the creators of those dances. This is why I doubt that even the most sincere students can recapture the Denishawn theatrical essence. Because steps were the least vital element in Denishawn works where the personalities of St. Denis, Shawn, and their Dancers were one with the choreography, in ensemble works and ballets as well as in solos.

The style and spirit of Ted Shawn's Americana dances can be more accurately passed on to young dancers than the St. Denis dances. I learned this in reconstructing his *Five American Sketches* (see pages 43–46) for the Vanaver Caravan to perform on the program celebrating the fiftieth anniversary of Jacob's Pillow. Although I no longer dance, I demonstrated sufficiently clearly for Bill Vanaver to state, in an interview about our work together, "The movement seemed very simple. But we were only able to grasp the *look* of the piece as it looked back then by really concentrating on observing Jane doing the movement today."

Once the steps had been memorized and the period and mood of each dance thoroughly understood, however, exhaustive work went into perfecting the required pantomime. For it had soon become obvious that dancers trained in modern schools to maintain expressionless faces in the studio, now had to be taught how to project characterizations that depended on acting (as did so many Denishawn dances). To their great credit, they learned admirably.

This suite had not been seen in its entirety by the general public since the Denishawn concert at Carnegie Hall on April 6, 1927. Its dances *(Danse Americaine, Around the Hall in Texas, A Gringo Tango, Pasquinade,* and *Boston Fancy: 1854)* blazed the trail for more sophisticated Americana, such as Martha Graham's *Appalachian Spring,* Doris Humphrey's *The Shakers,* Charles Weidman's *A Lincoln Portrait,* Eugene Loring's *Billy the Kid,* Jerome Robbins's *Fancy Free,* and Agnes de Mille's choreography for *Oklahoma!.* When Papa Denishawn's brief concert pieces are viewed from this historical perspective, therefore, they acquire an importance far beyond mere entertainment.

Allison Tracy wrote in the *Berkshire Eagle* of September 2, 1982, under a headline reading **Jacob's Pillow Hops Aboard the Revival Bandwagon:**

These dances have the naive charm of old silent films. As a picture is worth a thousand words, however, they can tell us more about our national origins in ten minutes than a day in the library poring over historical treatises. For the community at the Pillow, reconstruction emerged as a powerful teaching tool, a humbling artistic experience, and a way of building bridges across the generation gap.

In summary, I believe any revivalist of Denishawn works must emphasize the theatrical elements from which much of their quality derived. They must read and think about the cultural philosophies that influenced the creative impetus of St. Denis and Shawn, on which their choreography was based. They must have a sensitivity to music and a knowledge of imaginative lighting, costume, and makeup details. And they must have the integrity to try to comprehend and express the intent of each dance, as research into available sources reveals it.

In an article on revivals in the *New York Times* for April 13, 1980, Anna Kisselgoff hinted at this when she asked, "Is the spirit of a work less important than its steps?" To which I would reply, on behalf of Denishawn, "Approximate choreography staged by reconstructors and performed by dancers who had immersed themselves in a study of the era, the characters, and the theatrical-philosophical aspirations of St. Denis and Shawn can re-create a more faithful image of their dances than step-perfect revivals that ignore those factors. So devil take the steps! On with the show!"

Appendixes

Appendix I.
Partial Choreography

All the St. Denis and Shawn dances are solos unless otherwise indicated.

Dances on Religious Themes Created by Ruth St. Denis: 1906–1964

1906   *Radha*
        Incense

1907   *Yogi*

1910   *Isis* in *Egypta*

1913   *Bakawali* (ballet)

1915   *Garden of Kama* (first ballet choreographed with Ted Shawn)

1919   *Kuan Yin*

1922   *Egyptian Ballet* (choreographed with Ted Shawn)

1923   *Ishtar of the Seven Gates* (ballet)

1925   *Queen of Heaven: A Study of the Madonna*

1926   *Invocation to the Buddha*
        Soul of India
        White Jade

1927   *Kwannon*
        A Figure from Angkor Wat

1930   *A Buddhist Festival*
        Angkor Wat (ballet)

1935   *Masque of Mary*
        The Gold Madonna

1937   *Babylon*

1949   *Gregorian Chant* (with Rhythmic Choir)

1950s *Ballet of Christmas Hymns*
       Healing
       The Blue Madonna of St. Mark's
       Resurrection

1964   *Siddhas of the Upper Air* (duet with Ted Shawn, choreographed with
       Ted Shawn)

Dances on Religious Themes Created by Ted Shawn: 1915 – 1964

1915   *The Twenty-Third Psalm* (also known as *The Lord Is My Shepherd*)
       presented as part of *Three Dances of David (The Boy, the Shepherd,
       the King)*

       Joseph's Legend
       Garden of Kama (first ballet choreographed with Ruth St. Denis)

1917   *A Church Service in Dance Form*
       The Palms (to Gabriel Fauré's church music)

1919   *Miriam, Sister of Moses* (for Ruth St. Denis)
       Gnossienne (A Priest of Gnossos)

1920   *Les Mystères Dionysiaques* (Shawn with twelve dancers)

1921   *A Church Service in Dance Form* (Shawn with Martha Graham and
       two other dancers)
       Invocation to the Thunderbird

1922   *Egyptian Ballet* (choreographed with Ruth St. Denis)

1924   *Hopi Eagle Dance* (from the ballet *The Feather of the Dawn*)

1926   *The Cosmic Dance of Siva*

1929   *Mevlevi Dervish*
       Ramadan Dance
       Death of the Bull God (also known as *The Minotaur*)

1931   *Job* (ballet)

1932   *Methodist Revival Hymn* (from *Four Dances Based on American Folk
       Music*)

1933   *O Brother Sun and Sister Moon (A Study of St. Francis)*
       Negro Spirituals (for group)

1934   *The Hound of Heaven*

1935   *Brother Bernard, Brother Lawrence, Brother Masseo: Three Varieties
       of Religious Expression* (trio)

1939   *I Call Upon Thee, My Lord*
        Jésu, Joy of Man's Desiring (group)
        Isaiah 52:1–7 (group)
        The Divine Idiot

1964   *Siddhas of the Upper Air* (choreographed with Ruth St. Denis as their
        final duet)

Appendix II.
First independent program given by
Martha Graham, with
Thelma Biracree, Betty MacDonald,
and Evelyn Sabin
Louis Horst, Musical Director
The 48th Street Theatre,
New York City, April 18, 1926

Dance	Composer
Chorale	César Franck
Novelette	William Schuman
Tanze	Franz Schubert
Intermezzo	Johannes Brahms
Maid with the Flaxen Hair	Claude Debussy
First Arabesque	Claude Debussy
Clair de Lune	Claude Debussy
Danse Languide	Alexander Scriabin
Desire	Alexander Scriabin
Deux Valses Sentimentales	Maurice Ravel
Tanagra	Erik Satie
A Florentine Madonna	Sergei Rachmaninoff
Gnossienne	Erik Satie
A Study in Lacquer	Marcel Bernheim
Dance Rococo	Maurice Ravel
Marionette Show	Eugene Goossens
Gypsy Portrait	Manuel de Falla

Appendix III.
First independent program given by Doris Humphrey and Charles Weidman with their Student Concert Group Louis Horst, Pianist-Conductor Civic Repertory Theatre, New York City, October 28, 1928

Part I

Air for the G String   Music by J. S. Bach
Celia Rauch, Cleo Athenos, Evelyn Fields, Rose Yasgour, Sylvia Manning

Sarabande   Music by Rameau-Godowsky
Doris Humphrey

Scherzo   Music by Borodin
Charles Weidman

Color Harmony   Music by Clifford Vaughan
Dark Red: Geordie Graham, Virginia Landreth, Celia Rauch, Gertrude Shurr
Scarlet: Dorothy Lathrop, Sylvia Manning, Jean Nathan
Green: Cleo Athenos, Evelyn Fields, Jane Sherman, Rose Yasgour
Purple: Justine Douglas, Margaret Gardner, Eleanor King,
Katherine Manning
Violet: Leja Gorska
White: Charles Weidman

Part II

Papillon   Music by Rosenthal
Doris Humphrey

Water Study   Unaccompanied
Ensemble

Cathédrale Engloutie   Music by Debussy
Charles Weidman

Bagatelle   Music by Beethoven
Evelyn Fields and Sylvia Manning

Minstrels   Music by Debussy
Charles Weidman, John Glenn, Eugene LeSieur

First Movement of the Concerto in A Minor by Grieg for piano and orchestra
Doris Humphrey and Ensemble

Part III

Pavane of the Sleeping Beauty: Music by Ravel
The Fairy Garden
Doris Humphrey

Japanese Actor (XVII Century)   Music by Louis Horst
Charles Weidman

The Banshee   Music by Henry Cowell
Doris Humphrey

Ringside   Music by Winthrop Sargent
John Glenn and Charles Laskey

Étude (opus 8, no. 12)   Music by Scriabin
Doris Humphrey and Charles Weidman

Appendix IV.
Ted Shawn's choreographic notes for
Choeur Dansé, 1926
To music by the same name by
Vladimir Stcherbatcheff
First Performed July 15, 1926, at the
Victoria Theatre, Singapore

(Where "hops" are indicated, they are always done on high half-toe with knees in demi-plié.)

I (9/8 time) From lower stage Left, center girl (A) leaps, runs four steps, and holds pose on half-toe, looking back (1,2,3,4,5). Girls (B and C) one a little ahead of the other, arms arched overhead with hands clasped, hop on half-toe behind her (1,2,3,4) (ONE MEASURE). This is repeated (ONE MEASURE). A leaps and runs in back of others and holds pose. B and C hop (ONE MEA-SURE). A leaps and runs to Right and turns hips L, R, and holds pose, looking back. B and C walk R and face back, holding pose on half-toes (ONE MEA-SURE). A leaps to side and runs forward with little crossing steps and holds on toes, hands on head, palms front. B walks around C and holds, not loosing hands (ONE MEASURE). A repeats and leaps and runs forward and holds. C walks around B and holds (ONE MEASURE). A turns and runs back and holds, back to audience and arms high. B and C step and sway R into fifth: step and sway L into fifth (ONE MEASURE). A lifts in *attitude* as if calling and runs to lower L and kneels, hands out. B and C lift in *attitude* and follow, B into half-kneel and C a little higher (ONE MEASURE).

II (7/8 time) B and C, with an accent on count 1, rise and step briskly back six and hold on half toes, with arms crossed on breast (ONE MEASURE). A, with accent on count 1, rises and runs back six steps and holds, arms outstretched

(ONE MEASURE). B and C repeat and hold, arms out shoulder-high (ONE MEASURE). A repeats and runs back, finishing with arms crossed, hands on shoulder. B and C cross their arms in back of A and take her hands on her shoulders, their outside arms out (ONE MEASURE). All three make little leap on 1, and run to lower R (ONE MEASURE). Leap and run to L, keeping line flat to audience (ONE MEASURE). Hop four times on both half-toes, still in flat line. Break and run back three steps, leap, three steps, and turn, crouching close together in line facing R: weight on R toe, L foot behind R knee, and look over shoulder at audience (TWO MEASURES).

III (9/8 time) A sweeps a low rond de jambe with R leg and turns forward and holds pose. B and C hop four (ONE MEASURE). A repeats, swoops and holds. B and C hop four (ONE MEASURE). A leaps and runs R. B and C turning out away from each other make a coupé pirouette and an attitude pirouette (ONE MEASURE). All break and run to places: A center back, B and C at lower R and L (ONE MEASURE).

IV (7/8 time) All run to center five steps, make little back kick turning upper body away from center (ONE MEASURE). Spin four counts back toward place and run remaining three counts backward (ONE MEASURE). Repeat above two measures (TWO MEASURES). B and C run to center and fondé facing each other, inside hands joined (ONE MEASURE). A runs forward, leaps over the others' hands and all rise together on 7 (ONE MEASURE). Following each other, all sauté in and run six steps, leap and run around R in circle to back, center (TWO MEASURES).

V (9/8 time) B and C join inside hands over A's head: A takes their free hands in hers. On half-toes walk nine little steps to lower R (ONE MEASURE). All walk eight little steps to lower L. On 9 step on R foot (ONE MEASURE). Turn swiftly in place to face back, frightened, keeping weight on R. Look over L shoulder at audience. Three little jetés moving back, turn to face L, swinging R leg into arabesque. Drop forward on R into fondé, hands back to L, and looking back over R shoulder (FOUR MEASURES). Blackout. (Throughout dance, the lighting is a bright tawny rose.)

Appendix V.

Program by Ted Shawn and his Ensemble of Men Dancers at the Boston Repertory Theatre Tuesday, March 21, 1933 Jack Cole, Barton Mumaw, Sterling Stamford, Frank Overlees and Wilbur McCormack, with Springfield College students Seth Goodwin, Francis Luoma, George Panff, Peter Pretka, Clayton Shay, Clyde Schotzbarger, John Seeley and Lyle Welser Mary Campbell at the piano

1. *Osage-Pawnee Dance of Greeting* (Grunn)
   Msrs. Goodwin, Luoma, Panff, Pretka, Shay, Schotzbarger, Seeley, and Welser
   (See pps. 42–43)

2. *Invocation to the Thunderbird* (Sousa)
   Ted Shawn
   A prayer ritual for rain in which the dancer takes meal that has been blessed by the medicine-man and draws on the ground the pattern of the Thunderbird, the Indian Rain God, to end exulting in his successful magic. (For full description see pp. 28–29 of *The Drama of Denishawn Dance*.)

3. *Cutting the Sugar Cane* (Lecuona)
   Jack Cole, Barton Mumaw, Sterling Stamford, and Wilbur McCormack
   A dance inspired by the laborers in the sugar-cane fields, as Shawn had seen in Cuba. Dressed in white cotton ankle-length pants held up by red belts, and wearing wide-brimmed white straw hats, the four men entered on a diagonal from upstage left to downstage right, progressing with stylized movements

of cutting the cane, binding it into bundles, and throwing these into a pile at center. Resting from the heat and exertion, one of the men begins to dance in the middle of a circle formed by the others, all enjoying themselves until they see the (imaginary) overseer approaching. He whips them back to work. They repeat the opening labor themes and patterns with greater vigor until the end of the day, when three men walk off bearing bundles on their backs, leaving the fourth to dance a moment before shrugging his shoulders and leaping offstage after them.

4. *Charlie's Dance* (Haserodt)
   Ted Shawn
   A West Indian episode in which Charlie, while chasing butterflies, meets his sweetheart and learns that she is leaving him forever.

5. *Workers' Songs of Middle Europe* (Reinitz)
   Jack Cole, Barton Mumaw, Sterling Stamford, and Wilbur McCormack
   (a) *March of the Proletariat:* Four men, dressed only in dark work pants, form marching patterns with arm-thrusts that indicate the challenge of workers to their hard world.
   (b) *Who Would be a Shopkeeper, Bureaucrat or Soldier?* (Also known as "The Vagabonds' Song"): This was a dance in verse and chorus form, with each man in turn imitating a village character: the drunkard, the bureaucrat, the mayor, and the fat tavern-keeper. It ends with a rowdy pattern of laughter and ridicule of these prototypes.
   (c) *The Miller's Song: Work is Bread and without Work there is no Bread:* This opens with the men turning the wheel of a mill in back-breaking effort. They rest briefly, at intervals, then return to the work. It is somehow indicated that the mill shuts down, whereupon the workers go out to beg for help. Finding none, they threaten to destroy the mill, but the dance ends with the men in a hopeless mass, hands out-stretched.

6. *Flamenco Dances* (Spanish mss.)
   Ted Shawn

7. *Los Embozados* (Albeniz)
   Ted Shawn and Jack Cole, Barton Mumaw and Sterling Stamford
   The title means The Cloaked Ones. It applied to a gang of cutthroats, with Shawn as their "godfather." All wear black mohair pants, black shirts, black broad-brimmed Andalusian hats, and black boots. Each man is enveloped in a long black shoulder cape trimmed with a narrow edging of red. To the toccata-like music, the group moves in a tightly knit formation with heel beats that crescendo and decrescendo. They stop to plot their next robbery or murder. Enclosed in a circle of their capes, three plot against the Leader, but with much stomping of feet and whirling of capes, he wins them back. At

the end, they exit by skimming silently across the stage, their capes billowing behind them like black wings.

INTERMISSION

1. *Japanese Rickshaw Coolies* (Ganne)
   Jack Cole, Barton Mumaw, Wilbur McCormack
   Costumed in short dark blue workers' *hapi* coats with wide coral-colored *obis,* wearing flat, round straw hats, the men enter with smooth running suggestive of rickshaw pullers threading their vehicles through traffic. During a rest period, they gather to play a gambling game with finger symbols. One man is caught cheating and a laughing argument ensues. Then each man is hired again and all run offstage in different directions at the end of the dance.

2. *Japanese Spear Dance* (Horst)
   Ted Shawn
   (See pps. 39–40)

3. *Camel Boy* (Strickland)
   Jack Cole
   Dressed in full, ankle-length, baggy pants, the dancer wears a white turban and carries a six-foot-long whip with which he drives his camels to work. It is a gymnastic tour de force of exuberant leaps and turns and sharp, violent cracking of the whip against the floor.

4. *Gnossienne* (Satie)
   Barton Mumaw
   (See page 109)

5. *Rhapsody* (Brahms) Op. 119, No. 4
   Ted Shawn and Jack Cole, Barton Mumaw, Sterling Stamford, and Frank Overlees
   An abstract dance that follows the conventions of a musical quintet, with Shawn as soloist and the four men as accompanying instruments. The dancers wear only brief silk trunks, their almost nude bodies emphasizing the sculptural group formations made with powerful, free modern movements.

6. *Four Dances Based on American Folk Music*
   Ted Shawn
   (See pps. 46–47)

7. *Negro Spirituals* (traditional)

    (a) *Go Down, Moses*

    Jack Cole, Barton Mumaw, Sterling Stamford, and Frank Overlees

    (b) *Jacob's Ladder*

    Cole, Mumaw, Stamford, Overlees, and Wilbur McCormack

    (c) *Calvary*

    Ted Shawn and full company

These three works use forceful, abstract movements that suggest religious exultation and gain strength and intensity through the close unity and identical costuming of the group (see pps. 113–114).

Sources

Sources for Chapter 1

St. Denis, Ruth. "The Dance as Life Experience." *Denishawn Magazine*, 1 (1924).
——. *An Unfinished Life*. New York: Harper & Brothers, 1939.
Schlundt, Christena L. *The Professional Appearances of Ruth St. Denis and Ted Shawn: A Chronology and Index of Dances 1906–1932*. New York: New York Public Library, 1962.
Shawn, Ted. *The American Ballet*. New York: Henry Holt & Co., 1926.
——. *Gods Who Dance*. New York: E. P. Dutton, 1929.
——. *Every Little Movement: A Book about François Delsarte*. Pittsfield, Mass.: Eagle Printing Co., 1963.
Shawn, Ted, and Poole, Gray. *One Thousand and One Night Stands*. New York: Doubleday & Co., 1960.
Shelton, Suzanne. *Divine Dancer*. New York: Doubleday & Co., 1981.
Terry, Walter. *Miss Ruth*. New York: Dodd, Mead & Co., 1969.
——. *Ted Shawn: Father of the American Dance*. New York: Dial Press, 1976.

Sources for Chapter 2

Cohen, Barbara Naomi, ed. *The Franchising of Denishawn*. Dance Data No. 4. Brooklyn: Dance Horizons, 1979.
Cohen, Selma Jeanne (with Doris Humphrey). *Doris Humphrey: An Artist First*. Middletown, Conn.: Wesleyan University Press, 1972.
DeMille, Agnes. *Dance to the Piper*. New York: Little, Brown & Co., 1952.
Kanin, Garson. *Smash*. New York: Viking Press, 1980.
McDonagh, Don. Obituary of Ruth St. Denis. *New York Times*, July 22, 1968.
St. Denis, Ruth. *An Unfinished Life*. New York: Harper & Brothers, 1939.

Schlundt, Christena L. *The Professional Appearances of Ruth St. Denis and Ted Shawn: A Chronology and Index of Dances 1906–1932*. New York: New York Public Library, 1962.

Shawn, Ted, and Poole, Gray. *One Thousand and One Night Stands*. New York: Doubleday & Co., 1960.

Sherman, Jane. *The Drama of Denishawn Dance*. Middletown, Conn.: Wesleyan University Press, 1979.

——. *The Technique of Denishawn*, delivered at the State University of New York-Purchase Conference, *The Early Years: American Modern Dance from 1900 through the 1930s*, April 9–12, 1981.

——. *Soaring: The Diary and Letters of a Denishawn Dancer in the Far East: 1925–1926*. Middletown, Conn.: Wesleyan University Press, 1976.

Sources for Chapter 3

Sherman, Jane. *Soaring: The Diary and Letters of a Denishawn Dancer in the Far East: 1925–1926*. Middletown, Conn.: Wesleyan University Press, 1976.

——. Commemoration of Ruth St. Denis Day, May 16, 1981, Somerville, New Jersey.

Sources for Chapter 4

Archives of Jacob's Pillow, Kitty Cunningham, and Norton Owen.

Cohen, Barbara Naomi, ed. *The Franchising of Denishawn*. Dance Data No. 4. Brooklyn: Dance Horizons, 1979.

Dreier, Katherine S. *Shawn The Dancer*. New York: A. S. Barnes & Co., 1933.

Shawn, Ted, and Poole, Gray. *One Thousand and One Night Stands*. New York: Doubleday & Co., 1960.

Shelton, Suzanne. *Divine Dancer*. New York: Doubleday & Co., 1981.

Sherman, Jane. *The Drama of Denishawn Dance*. Middletown, Conn.: Wesleyan University Press, 1979.

Weidman, Charles. "Danse Americaine." In *Theatrical Dancing in America: The Development of the Ballet from 1900*, edited by Winthrop Palmer. New York: Bernard Ackerman, 1945.

Films courtesy of the Dance Collection, Library of Performing Arts, New York Public Library, New York.

(Note: For detailed descriptions of most of the dances mentioned in this chapter, and many more, see Jane Sherman, *The Drama of Denishawn Dance*, Middletown, Conn.: Wesleyan University Press, 1979.)

(For complete scenario of *Radha*, see Suzanne Shelton, *Divine Dancer*, New York: Doubleday & Co., pp. 59–65.)

Sources for Chapter 5

Baral, Robert. *Revue.* New York: Fleet Publishing Corp., 1962.

King, Eleanor. *Transformations.* Brooklyn: Dance Horizons, 1978.

Schlundt, Christena L. *The Professional Appearances of Ruth St. Denis and Ted Shawn: A Chronology and Index of Dances 1906–1932.* New York: New York Public Library, 1962.

Shawn, Ted, and Poole, Gray. *One Thousand and One Night Stands.* New York: Doubleday & Co., 1960.

Sherman, Jane. "A Denishawn Dancer with the Ziegfeld Follies." *Dance Magazine,* June, 1975.

———. *Denishawn in Vaudeville and Beyond,* delivered to C. W. Post College *Musical Theatre in America Conference,* April 1–5, 1981, at C. W. Post Center of Long Island University, Greenvale, New York.

Terry, Walter. *Miss Ruth.* New York: Dodd, Mead & Co., 1969.

———. Commemoration of Ruth St. Denis Day, May 16, 1981, Somerville, New Jersey.

Sources for Chapter 6

Shawn, Ted, and Poole, Gray. *One Thousand and One Night Stands.* New York: Doubleday & Co., 1960.

Sherman, Jane. *Soaring: The Diary and Letters of a Denishawn Dancer in the Far East: 1925–1926.* Middletown, Conn.: Wesleyan University Press, 1976.

———. "We Danced for the Nizam." *Dance Magazine,* February, 1976.

Sources for Chapter 7

Cohen, Selma Jeanne, and Humphrey, Doris. *An Artist First.* Middletown, Conn.: Wesleyan University Press, 1972.

Leatherman, Leroy. *Martha Graham.* New York: Alfred A. Knopf, 1966.

McDonagh, Don. *Martha Graham: A Biography.* New York: Praeger Publishers, 1973.

St. Denis, Ruth. *An Unfinished Life.* New York: Harper & Brothers, 1939.

Sherman, Jane. *The Drama of Denishawn Dance.* Middletown, Conn.: Wesleyan University Press, 1979.

———. "Doris and Charles and Pauline Fifty Years Ago." *Dance Magazine,* October, 1978.

Stodelle, Ernestine. *The First Frontier: The Story of Louis Horst and the American Dance.* Hastings-on-Hudson, N.Y.: private printing, 1964.

Wentink, Andrew. "Being an Idealist: Doris Humphrey's Letters Regarding Her Break with Ruth St. Denis and Ted Shawn." *Dance Magazine,* January, 1976.

Sources for Chapter 8

Brown, Jean Morrison, ed. *The Vision of Modern Dance.* Princeton, N.J.: Princeton Book Co., 1979.

Mumaw, Barton, and Sherman, Jane. *One Step at a Time: The Life of Barton Mumaw from the Men Dancers, Jacob's Pillow, Broadway and Beyond.* To be published by Dance Horizons.

———. "How it All Began: Ted Shawn's First Modern All-Male Dance Concert." *Dance Magazine,* July, 1982.

St. Denis, Ruth. *Lotus Light* (Poems). Cambridge, Mass.: Riverside Press, 1932.

———. "The Beleaguered City" (1949). Quoted in *The Performing Arts at UCLA* 13, no. 4, August 24, 1976.

Schlundt, Christena L. *The Professional Appearances of Ted Shawn and His Men Dancers: A Chronology and an Index of Dances 1933–1940.* New York: New York Public Library, 1967.

Shawn, Ted, and Poole, Gray. *One Thousand and One Night Stands.* New York: Doubleday & Co., 1960.

———. *Credo.* Private printing.

———. *Dance We Must.* Pittsfield, Mass.: Eagle Printing Co., 1940.

Shelton, Suzanne. *Divine Dancer.* New York: Doubleday & Co., 1981.

Sherman, Jane. *The Drama of Denishawn Dance.* Middletown, Conn.: Wesleyan University Press, 1979. (See pp. 33–34 for full description of *Gnossienne* mentioned in this chapter.)

Sherman, Jane, and Mumaw, Barton. "Ted Shawn: Teacher and Choreographer," *Dance Chronicle* 4, no. 2, 1981.

Denishawn Magazine (1924–1925).

Sources for Chapter 9

Louis, Murray. *Inside Dance.* New York: St. Martin's Press, 1980.

Sherman, Jane. "Denishawn Revisited." *Ballet Review* 9, no. 1, April, 1981.

———. *Thoughts on Reviving Denishawn.* Delivered to advanced class on modern dance given by Suzanne Shelton at New York University, June, 1981.

———. *Denishawn Revivals: One Method in the Madness.* Delivered at the State University of New York-New Paltz, Congress on Dance Research Conference, New Paltz, N.Y., October 8–11, 1982.

———. Letter to the Editor. *Smithsonian,* December, 1980.

Terry, Walter. "An Effort to Save the Masterpieces of Modern Dance." *Smithsonian,* October, 1980.

Selected Bibliography

Books

Baral, Robert. *Revue.* New York: Fleet Publishing Corp., 1962.

Brown, Jean Morrison, ed. *The Vision of Modern Dance.* Princeton, N.J.: Princeton Book Co., 1979.

Cohen, Barbara Naomi, ed. *The Franchising of Denishawn,* Dance Data No. 4. Brooklyn: Dance Horizons, 1979.

Cohen, Selma Jeanne, and Humphrey, Doris. *An Artist First.* Middletown, Conn.: Wesleyan University Press, 1972.

DeMille, Agnes. *Dance to the Piper.* New York: Little, Brown & Co., 1952.

Dreier, Katherine S. *Shawn The Dancer.* New York: A. S. Barnes & Co., 1933.

Kanin, Garson. *Smash.* New York: Viking Press, 1980.

King, Eleanor. *Transformations.* Brooklyn: Dance Horizons, 1978.

Leatherman, Leroy. *Martha Graham.* New York: Alfred A. Knopf, 1966.

Louis, Murray. *Inside Dance.* New York: St. Martin's Press, 1980.

McDonagh, Don. *Martha Graham: A Biography.* New York: Praeger Publishers, 1973.

St. Denis, Ruth. *An Unfinished Life.* New York: Harper & Brothers, 1939.

———. *Lotus Light* (Poems). Cambridge, Mass.: Riverside Press, 1932.

Schlundt, Christena L. *The Professional Appearances of Ruth St. Denis and Ted Shawn: A Chronology and Index of Dances 1906–1932.* New York: New York Public Library, 1962.

———. *The Professional Appearances of Ted Shawn and His Men Dancers: A Chronology and Index of Dances 1933–1940.* New York: New York Public Library, 1967.

Shawn, Ted. *The American Ballet.* New York: Henry Holt & Co., 1926.

———. *Credo.* Private printing ca. 1970.

———. *Dance We Must.* Pittsfield, Mass.: Eagle Printing Co., 1940.

———. *Every Little Movement: A Book about François Delsarte.* Pittsfield, Mass.: Eagle Printing Co., 1963.

———. *Gods Who Dance.* New York: E. P. Dutton Co., 1929.

———. *How Beautiful upon the Mountain.* Private printing, 1943.

———. *The Story of Jacob's Pillow.* Private printing.

Shawn, Ted, and Poole, Gray. *One Thousand and One Night Stands.* New York: Doubleday & Co., 1960.

Shelton, Suzanne. *Divine Dancer.* New York: Doubleday & Co., 1981.

Sherman, Jane. *The Drama of Denishawn Dance.* Middletown, Conn.: Wesleyan University Press, 1979.

———. *Soaring: The Diary and Letters of a Denishawn Dancer in the Far East: 1925–1926.* Middletown, Conn.: Wesleyan University Press, 1976.

Stodelle, Ernestine. *The First Frontier: The Story of Louis Horst and the American Dance.* Hastings-on-Hudson, N.Y.: private printing, 1964.

Terry, Walter. *Miss Ruth.* New York: Dodd, Mead & Co., 1969.

———. *Ted Shawn: Father of the American Dance.* New York: Dial Press, 1976.

Unpublished and Miscellaneous Sources

Choreographic notes and other pertinent material by and about Ruth St. Denis and Ted Shawn at the University of California at Los Angeles; similar material and films in the Denishawn Collection, Dance Collection, Library & Museum of the Performing Arts, New York Public Library (Lincoln Center); correspondence between Ted Shawn and Lucien Price; archives of Jacob's Pillow.

Correspondence and/or conversations with the author by Louise Brooks, Anne Douglas, Geordie Graham, Barton Mumaw, Ted Shawn, Suzanne Shelton, Gertrude Shurr, and Walter Terry.

Souvenir programs, theatre programs, diary, letters, choreographic notes, music, classroom notes, photographs, and newspaper clippings in the author's personal collection.

Index

𝒜

Adagio Pathétique (Shawn), (See Death of Adonis, The)

Adelphi University, 104

Ailey, Alvin, 30, 105, 127

Album Leaf and Prelude (Shawn), 81, 98

Allegresse (Shawn), 67

America Dancing (John Martin), quoted, 121

Americana, 21, 36, 41–47, 128, 133

Ampico Player Piano Co., 20

An Artist First (Doris Humphrey, with Selma Jeanne Cohen), 89

Anderson, John Murray, 86

Anderson, Lily Strickland, 21, 41

Andrews, Florence, (See O'Denishawn, Florence)

Annie Get Your Gun, 66

Appalachian Spring (Graham), 133

Arabic Duet (Shawn), 88

Arabic Suite (Shawn), 8

Around the Hall in Texas (Shawn), 21, 45, 66, 82, 133

Art of Making Dances, The (Humphrey), 17

Austin, Anna, 28, 104

Austin, Ruth, 89, 98

ℬ

Balanchine, George, 65, 128

Bales, William, 101

Ballet of Ancient Egypt, (See Egypta)

Ballets Russes, 14, 55

Barnes, Clive, 94

Baryshnikov, Mikhail, 127

Basket Dance, The (St. Denis), 24

Beethoven, Ludwig van, 48

Belasco, David, 5

Beleaguered City, The (St. Denis), quoted, 124

Berkshire Eagle, The, quoted, 133

Bernhardt, Sarah, 63

Beyer, Hilda, 8

Billy the Kid (Loring), 133

Body in Question, The (Dr. Jonathan Miller), quoted, 115

Bond, Carrie Jacobs, 42

Boston Fancy: 1854 (Shawn), 21, 66, 75, 82, 83, 133

Boston Globe, The, quoted, 123, 124

Boston Herald, The, quoted, 121

Boston Repertory Theatre, 112

Bourmann, Anatole, 111, 112

Bourrée (Humphrey), 95

Bowen, Dorothea, 48, 56

Braggiotti, Berthe, 18

About the Author

JANE SHERMAN STUDIED AT THE NEW YORK Denishawn School from 1923 to 1925. As the youngest member of the Denishawn Dancers, she then joined Ruth St. Denis and Ted Shawn for their epochmaking tour of the Orient in 1925–1926, for the United States tour of 1926–1927, and for the *Ziegfeld Follies* tour of this country in 1927–1928. She was a member of the first Humphrey-Weidman Company in 1928–1929, after which she appeared in several Broadway musicals and, for a year and a half, danced as a Rockette at Radio City Music Hall.

She is the author of *Soaring: The Diary and Letters of a Denishawn Dancer in the Far East: 1925–1926,* published by Wesleyan University Press in 1976, for which she was awarded the de la Torre Bueno Prize; and of *The Drama of Denishawn Dance,* written with the help of a grant from the National Endowment for the Humanities and published by Wesleyan University Press in 1979. With Barton Mumaw, she is co-author of *One Step at a Time,* a book on his life, the building of Jacob's Pillow, the tours of Shawn's Men Dancers, and beyond to Shawn's death in 1972, to be published by Dance Horizons.

In 1981, she revived Ted Shawn's *Boston Fancy: 1854* for performance by the Vanaver Caravan at Jacob's Pillow. She has also revived St. Denis music visualizations for the New Jersey Center of the Performing Arts and The Dancemakers of St. Petersburg, Florida. As part of the Jacob's Pillow Fiftieth Anniversary celebrations, she presented the Vanaver Caravan in her reconstruction of Shawn's *Five American Sketches,* August, 1982.